Food & Folklore of the 1,000 Islands

Savor the Flavor of the Islands

Volume I

Pamela & Michael Sykes

Sykes, Pamela, 1951 –
    Food & folklore of the 1,000 Islands : savor
the flavor of the islands

1st ed.
Includes bibliographical references.
ISBN 1-896395-00-7 (v. 1)

    1. Cookery–Thousand Islands (N.Y. and Ont.).
2. Thousand Islands (N.Y. and Ont.) – History
3. Restaurants – Thousand Islands (N.Y. and Ont.).
I. Sykes, Michael, 1944–   . II. Title.
III. Title: Food and folklore of the 1,000
Islands.

TX715.6.S94 1995   641.59713'7   C95-900166-2

Published by:
    Dove Cottage Press
    160 Georgiana Street
    Gananoque, Ontario, Canada K7G 1M7

Willows whiten, aspens quiver,
Little breezes duck and shiver
Thro' the wave that runs for ever
By the island in the river
        Flowing down to Camelot.

THE LADY OF SHALOTT
ALFRED LORD TENNYSON

Cover Photo: Parks Canada — Sunset near Camelot Island, 1,000 Islands

PRINTED IN CANADA

Acknowledgements

This book could not exist without the encouragement and generosity of its contributors. To the restaurant owners, chefs and home-based cooks who shared their secrets, we express heartfelt thanks.

As believers in The Golden Rule (the person with the gold makes the rules), we thank our 'golden ruler' — banker-business advisor par excellence, Paul Hodgert of the Brockville Leeds Business Development Corporation.

While speaking of things golden, we are grateful to Shirley Fernetich of The Golden Apple Restaurant.

To Stewart Renfrew and Don Richan of the Queen's University Archives, thank you for your patience and direction. To Sandra Bell of The National Library in Ottawa, thank you for the wealth of information. To John Love of Gananoque Public Library, and his librarian wife Barbara, thank you for responding with good humor to our many annoying, and occasionally weird requests for information over the years.

To Macintosh guru Larry MacMillan, thank you for illuminating some electronic esoterica. To Ralph Smith, thank you for sharing your memories. Special thanks to Mary Joan Barrett who kindly permitted us to publish recipes from her excellent book, *In Praise of Pumpkins*. Curator David St. Onge of the Correctional Service of Canada Museum earned our gratitude by identifying a Kingston Penitentiary female prisoner who was mentioned in a 19th century diary.

We express our heartfelt thanks to those who trusted us with family histories and personal reminiscences.

A special 'thank you' goes to Francis Loughheed of Loughheed and Associates of Belleville. He led us to a mountain top and revealed a vision of tomorrow.

Others unwittingly have contributed to this book. Into this category fall Bob Hilderley and Susan Hannah of Kingston's Quarry Press.

Evening

One solitary bird melodiously
    Trilled its sweet vesper from a grove of elm,
One solitary sail upon the sea
    Rested, unmindful of its potent helm.

And down behind the forest trees the sun,
    Arrayed in burning splendours, slowly rolled,
Like to some sacrificial urn, o'errun
    With flaming hues of crimson, blue and gold.

The fisher ceased his song, hung on his oars,
    Pausing to look, a pulse in every breath,
And, in imagination, saw the shores
    Elysian, rising o'er the realms of Death.

And down on tiptoe came the gradual night,
    A gentle twilight first, with silver wings,
And still from out the darkening infinite
    Came shadowy forms, like day's imaginings.

There was no light in all the brooding air,
    There was no darkness yet to blind the eyes,
But through the space interminable, there
    Nature and silence passed in solemn guise.

CHARLES SANGSTER
1822-1893
BORN IN KINGSTON, ONTARIO

Preface

Most of our life-altering decisions have been reached on our boat, anchored somewhere amidst the 1,000 Islands. One grey Sunday afternoon in November, we sprawled on Aubrey Island's dock and watched a gourmet serve himself lunch as we planned this cookbook.

The gourmet was a muskrat in search of succulent water plant roots, oblivious to the 'great' matters under discussion. That struck us as unusual; muskrats are the most circumspect critters. We interpreted this as a favorable omen because people keep asking ... why a cookbook?

Neither one of us likes to cook. It is safe to say that neither of us knows anything about cooking. So ... why? No great mystery, we love to eat. This cookbook contains recipes from our favorite restaurants and from people with excellent reputations as cooks in several 1,000 Islands communities.

Also, we both enjoy the written word, the splendor of the 1,000 Islands and its epicurean muskrats, and historical anecdotes. So we combined our love of food, books, nature and history. If you have to work, and we do, it is much more fun to work at something you enjoy. Hence this book which, presumptuously, we label Volume I.

Truly, this cookbook is different. Not only does it contain historical vignettes, it reveals the secret recipes of some of the 1,000 Islands area's best restaurants. All recipes have been set in larger-than-normal type to make them easier to read as you cook. We feel obliged to confess that time has precluded us from trying *every* recipe. But we can say that every recipe we tried has produced delightful meals and impressed guests, especially those who have seen our kitchen sign which exhorts us to "Just say 'NO' to cooking".

If these recipes can make us appear to be competent cooks, imagine what they can do for you.

Enjoy.

PAMELA & MICHAEL SYKES
1,000 ISLANDS
JANUARY 1995

Table of Contents

GREAT
EXPECTATIONS

River Rat's Revenge

Presented by The Lobster Trap Seafood Restaurant
650 King Street East, Gananoque

Editors' Note:

A word of explanation: a River Rat does not have four legs and a tail. A River Rat is a person, a title or honorific, awarded — not appropriated — by tradition, heritage and general knowledge of the St. Lawrence River.

We thought this excellent elixir might assist you in arriving at the proper frame of mind to enter the kitchen and cook.

Ingredients:

1 oz of white rum	1/2 oz of cocoanut rum
1/2 oz of banana liqueur	pineapple juice
cherry juice	orange slice
stemmed Maraschino cherry	

Method:

In a 10 oz cocktail glass filled with ice cubes, add the liquors. Then top up the glass with pineapple juice leaving enough room to stir in cherry juice until the drink has a rosy-red color. Garnish with a half slice of orange and a cherry.

Administer therapeutically by means of a straw.

The Lobster Trap Seafood Restaurant and Days Inn are owned by the Brown family. Day to day operations are in the hands of Syd, Gordon and Jeffrey Brown. Assistant manager and advocate of River Rat's Revenge is Ross Hamilton. The Lobster Trap is Gananoque's only seafood restaurant and offers daily specials including an Early Bird menu. Décor is definitely nautical and must be experienced to be believed. The cozy bar is named The Rum Runner Lounge.

Border? What border?

Canadians and Americans living by the St. Lawrence River have long been indifferent to the international border. They have crossed it to visit, intermarry and trade for 300 years. It was only natural that Canadians did not stand idly by during America's 13 years of sobriety called Prohibition from 1920 to 1933.

Selfless Canadian entrepreneurs labored mightily by moonlight to maintain refreshment levels south of the border. That some amassed fortunes in the process in no way detracts from their altruism. These heroes of capitalism were called Rum Runners. A suspicion lingers that Canadian distillers also may have accrued a benefit or two.

Fact or fiction?

The story of Oscar of the Waldorf and 1,000 Islands Salad Dressing is but one of the tall tales spun for the benefit of visitors. Another concerns 'the world's shortest international bridge'.

South of the picturesque village of Rockport lies Zavicon Island. In fact, there are two islands linked by a very short bridge. Tour operators suggest the bridge crosses the Canada-US boundary and is, therefore, the world's shortest international bridge.

But check a nautical chart and you will discover that Zavicon's Islands are a coin toss north of the international border. Still, it's a quaint tale.

However, there really is a very short international bridge; it is part of the 1,000 Islands International Bridge system. At one point, the countries are separated by a narrow water body called The International Rift, spanned by — you guessed it, a very short international bridge.

1,000 Islands Salad Dressing
Presented by: No One Knows For Sure

One 1,000 Islands tall tale credits Oscar, of New York's Waldorf Astoria Hotel fame, with creating 1,000 Islands Salad Dressing ... not true! Folks here like to claim that Oscar was steward or chef to hotel magnate George Boldt (he of Boldt Castle fame). During an 1890's islands cruise, the steward surpassed himself with the new salad dressing. Delighted, Boldt is said to have named it 1,000 Islands Dressing and decreed that it be served at his hotels.

In a fairy tale ending, the steward was promoted to work at Boldt's hotel and achieved international fame as Oscar of the Waldorf. In fact, Oscar Tschirky was famous — as a maitre d'hotel. His name is associated with certain dishes, but 1,000 Islands Dressing is not one of them according to The Waldorf Astoria Corporation which proclaims proud ownership of such famous recipes as Waldorf Salad.

Further, as maitre d', Oscar's presence was unlikely during that long ago 1,000 Islands cruise of discovery. In his autobiography, Oscar claims never to have visited the 1,000 Islands. At best, The Waldorf Astoria Corporation allows that 'someone' in Boldt's employ 'probably' created the popular salad dressing. But not Oscar. Nevertheless, the fairy tale version is still cited as gospel in the 1,000 Islands almost a century later. Who really created 1,000 Islands Dressing? No one, it seems, knows for sure.

Ingredients:

1 cup of mayonnaise	1 tsp of chopped green pepper
3 (or more) tbsp of chili sauce	1 tsp of chopped green olives
1 tsp of chopped pimiento	1 chopped hard-boiled egg
1 tsp of chopped chives	salt and pepper to taste

Method:
Mix ingredients and chill. Serves four.

Fish "Moqueca"

Presented by The Ivy Lea Resort & Marina, Ivy Lea

Ingredients:

4 tomatoes, cut up	1 red pepper, cut up
1 onion, cut into rings	1 tbsp of chopped fresh coriander
1 tbsp of chopped green onion	2 tbsp of oil
2 tbsp of tomato paste	1 tbsp of lemon juice
salt	pepper
4 lb of fish, preferably doré*, cut in slices	
1 lb of small shrimp, shelled and deveined	

*Doré, also known as walleye or yellow pickerel

Method:

Mix all ingredients, except the shrimp, and marinate for two hours. Preheat oven to 350°F. Place everything except the shrimp in a 13" by 9" glass baking dish, cover with aluminum foil and bake for 25 minutes. Remove from oven and add shrimp. Return to the oven for 10 minutes until the shrimp are cooked. Makes 6 to 8 servings. Serve over rice.

Under new management, the Ivy Lea Resort & Marina is located in the heart of the 1,000 Islands. The dining room seats 75 comfortably and provides a riverside view of the dramatic sunsets common in this area. An outdoor patio seats another 75. Canadian cuisine is featured and reservations are recommended on weekends and during the summer months. The resort presides over 35 acres of spectacular, natural setting and includes a large marina.

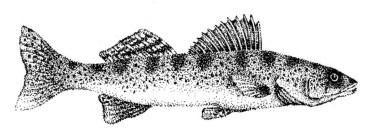

History and hospitality

Captain E.W. Visger launched a boat line and a tradition of ferrying visitors to the islands back in 1874. Among his vessels was the 116-foot New Island Wanderer, built at Buffalo and brought into service in 1888. She was known for her 50-mile cruises and night time searchlight excursions through the islands.

The New Island Wanderer's sister ships were the Captain Visger and the Castanet. The Castanet operated from the Ivy Lea Resort and many flocked there to cruise the famous 1,000 Islands.

Built late in the 19th century, this historic resort is located in the heart of the Navy Group of islands near the picturesque village of Ivy Lea.

Today, Captain Visger's tradition continues as a variety of tour boat lines ferry hundreds of thousands of visitors on island cruises.

3

1,000 Islands Shore Dinner

Presented by Tom Harrison, Gananoque's Gourmet Guide

A heritage meal

Railway barons and captains of industry visited the international playground that was the 1,000 Islands during the latter part of the 19th century. They came to challenge the mighty muskellunge or his clever cousin, the northern pike. Eventually, the islands attracted so many visitors that fishing lodges and hotels sprang up to accommodate them. Every morning, steam launches towed a string of skiffs to the best fishing grounds.

Hungry fishermen gathered at lunchtime to swap fish stories while their guides prepared feasts that centered on the morning's catch. Today's fishing guides maintain the tradition known as the shore dinner.

Editors' Note:

The shore dinner is a traditional feast which fishing guides serve to their customers. The tradition dates from the latter part of the 19th century. Be prepared to invest about 3 hours to do this properly.

Ingredients:

sliced bacon	fish (caught that morning)
sliced or "hunked up" potatoes	butter
shortening	salt and pepper to taste
parsley	sliced tomatoes
steak	bread
eggs	milk
ground coffee	vegetables for salad
salad dressing	assorted pies
flour	

Method:

Cook the potatoes in an iron frying pan which contains butter, shortening, salt, pepper and parsley. In another iron frying pan, fry some bacon while you make a salad with a side order of sliced tomatoes. Serve the bacon with fresh bread and the salad.

Add a little butter to the hot bacon grease. Dredge the fish filets in flour mixed with salt and pepper to taste and fry over a hot flame. Serve when golden brown. Next, cook a small steak over an open wood fire ... a barbecue is acceptable only if you live on the 40th floor of a highrise.

Continued on the next page

Continued from the previous page

Dip bread into an egg wash which contains very little milk to make French toast (see following recipe). It is traditional and acceptable to add a dash of scotch to taste.

In a bowl, add a few drops of water to coffee grounds and mix to form a paste while a kettle of water boils. To the paste, add an egg, shell included, and a dash of salt. Pour this mixture directly into the boiling water. Serve the coffee with the French toast.

Dessert follows for those with any vestige of an appetite remaining.

Tom Harrison has fished the St. Lawrence River and inland lakes for more than 50 years. He is one of the few remaining rivermen who earns his entire living on the St. Lawrence. He operates a water taxi, builds and repairs docks and looks after 19 island cottages. His son, Mark, works with him. Tom and Mark epitomize the River Rat title which Tom defines as: "a person who spends as much of his or her free time and waking hours as possible on the river."

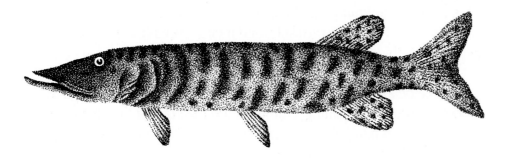

Fishy memories

Tom Harrison recalls a special day, long ago, when he and a friend caught 72 pike ... and released every one. They practised 'catch and release' before it became popular.

Another memory: May 5th, the opening day of the pike season, some 40 years ago, fishing from a dock in Gananoque. It began to snow.

"I think we caught 15 pike and four inches of snow that afternoon. It was wicked."

But he fished until dark. A true River Rat is undeterred by a little snow, even in May.

As a young lad, Tom worked for the owner of Dumbfounder Island. "My main job in the morning was to make toast over an open fire and that was how I got started on my cooking." Oddly, while Tom cooks exquisite fish dishes, he does not enjoy the taste of fish.

A secret revealed

The late George Dickson, a St. Lawrence River fishing guide, made French toast unlike any other, but he refused to share his recipe. In the words of family friend, Kate Phillips:

"His wife, Doreen, and I asked repeatedly, what made the difference? George always avoided answering. We tried spying. We tried 'borrowing' his battered, blackened, long-handled cast iron skillet when he wasn't around. We enlisted the aid of my mother-in-law who had been one of his fishing clients for donkey's years: 'My goodness, George, what makes your French toast so different and delicious'?"

Like a cagey muskie, George never rose to the bait.

Years later, Ms. Phillips snooped in the guide's lunch hamper. She discovered the secret ingredients were cinnamon, dark brown sugar and — believe it or not — crumpled newspaper. The secret recipe is reproduced on this page.

6

Shore Dinner French Toast
Presented by Kate Phillips & Doreen Dickson Glasser

Ingredients:

4 slices of Italian or homemade white bread sliced 1/2" thick
6 or 8 thick cut slices of bacon and a heavy iron skillet
1 double sheet newspaper crumpled to the size of a large fist
1/2 level tsp of cinnamon   dash of salt
4 rounded tsp of dark brown sugar   3 large eggs
1 1/2+ cups of milk   butter — 1/4 to 3/4 stick as required
maple syrup

Method:

Fry the bacon and drain on a paper towel. Beat the eggs, add salt and cinnamon and blend well. Add milk and beat until blended. Dip the bread, one slice at a time, into the egg and milk mixture and stack on a high rimmed plate. Pour the bacon fat from the skillet but leave a fine film in the pan. Wipe the skillet not quite clean with the crumpled newspaper. This does make a difference. Put a generous wedge of butter in the skillet and melt it over a low fire. When the butter begins to bubble, place the bread into the pan.

Dust one rounded teaspoon of brown sugar over each slice and dampen with any egg and milk mixture remaining. Carefully raise the edge of the bread to see if it is turning brown. When golden brown, slide the spatula under each slice scraping the bottom of the pan so the coating remains on the bread. Add butter to the skillet and raise each turned slice so butter melts under it. When both sides are cooked golden brown, serve with bacon and maple syrup.

Kate Phillips, now on her fourth career, enjoyed success as a featured player in film and on stage from 1935 through 1943, as a writer from 1945 to 1980, and as a teacher since 1970. Today she is the founder of the Gananoque Community Performing Arts Center.

Doreen Dickson Glasser met and married Dennis Glasser ten years after George Dickson's death. They live in Gananoque and are members of several Ontario craft guilds.

Ross Griffin's Fried Bullheads
Presented by Ross Griffin, Marble Rock Road

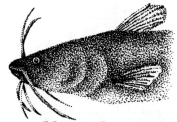

Catfish are called bullheads in the 1,000 Islands.

Editors Note:
You may wish to compare Tommy Harrison's shore dinner (pages 4 & 5) to Ross Griffin's version. Select the best of both, or whatever appeals to your own taste. Ross boils potatoes; Tommy fries his. Sometimes Ross cooks hamburgers, pork chops or even chicken instead of steak which Tommy serves. Ross makes his coffee by simply adding it to boiling water "and when it boils over 2 or 3 times I take it off the heat". Some of his customers call it Cowboy Coffee, regardless, it's great.

Ingredients:

bacon	shortening
flour	salt and pepper to taste
fresh bullheads	

Method:
Over a very hot burner, or open fire, fry the bacon and remove from pan. Mix some shortening with the bacon grease. Dredge the bullheads in the flour mixed with salt and pepper to taste. Place the floured fish into the hot grease/shortening mixture and fry. Turn once only; this is important. Serve when golden brown.

Ross Griffin has worked for more than 55 years as a fishing guide on Gananoque Lake. And for 30 of those years he was a commercial fisherman. Rest assured that he knows fish. In the words of a happy customer: "If you haven't had one of Ross Griffin's shore dinners, you haven't lived!" He guides from Griffin's Lakeside Cottages and Lodge on Gananoque Lake, owned and operated by his cousins, Ernie and Lew Griffin. Today, Ross guides part-time but he still finds time to take his great-granddaughter fishing.

Marble Rock memories

Ross Griffin no longer guides fishing parties every day, as he once did. Those fortunate few he does guide are familiar friends who have, for years, exploited his knowledge of Gananoque Lake to the disadvantage of its finned residents.

Ross says that some of his more serious clients will not use wire leaders for live or artificial bait. They claim that it retards the bait's action. One client, with an aversion to wire leaders, has a standing order each year for 10 spoons. And he loses them all because of his refusal to use a wire leader ... but he catches fish. And that's the game.

Ross encourages his clients to practise 'catch and release', keeping no more than an occasional pike or bass to enjoy at the traditional shore dinner.

Ross has a special talent. He can skin four bullheads in one minute. Impressive, but he knows someone else who can manage six.

Killer cures of yore

The following excerpts are taken from The Home Cook Book *compiled by The Ladies of Toronto and Chief Cities and Towns in Canada, 70th edition, 1877. It contains observation on social conventions as well as recipes. Here is a 19th century cold formula ... needless to say we do not recommend it. Well, maybe with a little tonic ...?*

"One pound of liverwort put into four quarts of water and boiled down to one quart; add, while warm, a quarter pound of ball liquorice and a quarter pound of loaf sugar; when cool add a half pint of gin. Dose – half a large wineglass half an hour before each meal."

And this to restore a victim of a lightning strike: "Shower with cold water for two hours; if the patient does not show signs of life, put salt in the water, and continue to shower an hour longer."

Rosy French Toast
Presented by The Victoria Rose Inn, 279 King Street West, Gananoque

Ingredients:

1 egg	1 cup of milk
1/2 tsp of vanilla	1 tsp of sugar
1/4 tsp of cinnamon	butter

4 oz of raspberry flavored cream cheese
8 slices of thick bread, either white or whole wheat

Method:

Using a fork, beat together the egg, milk, vanilla, sugar and cinnamon. Split the bread in half to create an envelope. Soften the cream cheese in a microwave oven for 15 seconds. Spread 1/8th of the cream cheese between the two halves of bread and press firmly together to seal. Repeat this with the other 7 slices.

Dip each slice quickly into the egg mixture and make sure the bread is well covered. Melt 1 tbsp of butter in a pan and sauté the bread on both sides. Cut in half, sprinkle with icing sugar and serve with maple syrup.

Variations:

Any kind of fruit flavored cream cheese may be used. When fresh fruit is in season, add 1/2 tsp of sugar to plain cream cheese, spread on the bread, sprinkle with raspberries, blueberries or other fruit, press very firmly to seal and cook as above.

Ric and Liz Austin are your hosts at The Victoria Rose Inn which is surrounded by two acres of gardens. This is a wonderful place for a wedding, party or meeting. Inside are five Italian marble fireplaces and period furnishings. Tea is served in the garden during the summer months. This impressive building was built in 1872 for Gananoque's first mayor, William Byers. Samuel McCammon purchased it in 1876 and named it Glenwood. *Next came the Bulloch family who lived there until the 1950's. Eventually, it was divided into apartments and named* The UN Inn *by Gananoque residents. It was renovated and restored to its 19th century grandeur in the mid-1980's.*

Niagara Peach and Blueberry French Toast

Presented by The Clarence Street Grill, 6 Clarence Street, Kingston

Ingredients:

4 thick slices, whole wheat bread	2 large eggs
1/4 cup of milk	2 tbsp of butter
4 oz of softened cream cheese	1 large or 2 small ripe peaches
2 handfuls of blueberries*	1 to 2 oz of Amaretto
icing sugar	pinch of cinnamon and nutmeg
toasted, sliced almonds (optional)	

*frozen berries may be used if fresh are unavailable

Method:

Make two sandwiches with the bread using the softened cream cheese as filling.

For the batter, beat the eggs, milk, cinnamon and nutmeg together. Slice the peaches and sauté over medium heat in butter until slightly soft. Add the blueberries and amaretto; let simmer for a minute or so.

Dip the sandwiches into the egg batter and cook until golden brown and crispy. Transfer to a warmed plate and slice on the diagonal. Pour fruit over top of the toast. Garnish with a sprinkling of icing sugar and toasted almonds.

Serves 2.

The Clarence Street Grill is owned by Leslie Leacy and Mark Smith and specializes in nouvelle cuisine. Sunday brunch, lunches and dinners are served. In season, enjoy the view of Kingston's harbor from an outdoor patio. Art posters and plants contribute to a feeling of casual elegance.

Fortress Kingston

The Shoal Tower, erected in 1846 as part of the British defence strategy for the city of Kingston, is one of four such Martello towers still standing.

The Martello Towers, in conjunction with Fort Henry, were designed to reinforce each other by setting up a crossfire upon any naval intruder trying to enter the Kingston Harbor or Rideau Canal. Each tower mounted cannon under a collapsible roof.

Improving Kingston's defences was deemed prudent because of the Oregon Crisis of 1846 which began as a western border dispute between the US and Britain's Canadian colony.

War was averted by diplomacy and by 1850 the Shoal Tower was pressed into service for barracks for soldiers of the Royal Canadian Rifles and their families.

Free trade is not new

The Canada Trade Act of 1822 slapped tariffs on American agricultural products. But wily American farmers herded pigs and oxen onto rafts used to transport timber down the St. Lawrence River. Perhaps some of these same pigs and oxen may have disembarked by moonlight along the Canadian shore without tariff revenue accruing to officialdom.

Changing seasons facilitated commerce. Americans drove livestock across the winter ice on the St. Lawrence River and Canadians, in search of deals, snapped up pork, flour and whisky at bargain prices. A century later the whisky tide turned as Canadians smuggled liquor into the US in defiance of Prohibition.

"... there is not a family of consequence in Canada which, by intermarriage or otherwise, has not relatives or dear personal friends across the border," wrote an Englishman in 1862.

St. Lawrence Fish Chowder
Presented by Caiger's Resort & Fishing Lodge, Rockport

Ingredients:

2 or 3 lb of fresh fish	1/4 to 1/2 cup of flour
salt and pepper to taste	Worcestershire sauce to taste
carrots	potatoes
onions	any other vegetables if preferred

Method:

Cook the cleaned, fresh fish in water until it is flakey. Remove from the water and cool.

To the fish stock, add as many vegetables as you like: small cubed carrots, potatoes and onions, for example, and cook until they are soft. Meanwhile, debone the fish. When the vegetables are cooked, add the fish to the stock and vegetables.

Add milk until you have enough to give you a hearty serving. Thicken with flour mixed with milk. Add salt and pepper and Worcestershire sauce to taste. Do not stir too much; the fish should be in small chunks.

Caiger's Resort & Fishing Lodge is owned and operated by the Spafford family. This recipe belonged to Ann Caiger who, with her husband Frank, established the lodge in 1945. Her daughter, Margaret Spafford, operates the lodge with her husband, Gordon. Margaret has improved the recipe. Caiger's has enjoyed a reputation throughout the 1,000 Islands for excellent dining since 1945.

Pasta Comforta

Presented by Greg Burliuk, "Great Gusto" Columnist
The Whig-Standard, Kingston

Ingredients:

1 lb of hot Italian sausage	2 tbsp of virgin olive oil
1 chopped medium onion	1/2 cup of mushrooms (optional)
1 tbsp of butter	1 chopped red pepper
4 garlic cloves, chopped	dried chilies to taste
1/2 cup of red wine vinegar	2 fistfuls of uncooked linguine

Method:

Slice the sausage and brown it in the olive oil over medium heat (250°F if you have an electric frying pan). Add the onion and cook until golden then add the mushrooms. When water for the pasta is boiling, add the linguine and at the same time add the butter and red pepper to the sausage mixture.

When the pasta is nearly done, add the garlic and chilies to the sausages. Drain the pasta. Add the wine vinegar to the sausages and use it to scrape brown bits off the bottom of the pan, then turn off the heat. Add the pasta to the pan and use it to sop up all the juices from the pan.

Serves two hungry people after a long, troublesome week at work.

For the last three years, Greg Burliuk has been writing Great Gusto *for the Saturday edition of Kingston's Whig-Standard. His column celebrates food and food makers in the Kingston area. In the process, Greg has learned the mysteries of poutine, thickened his waist-line and tasted the fare at a legion of local restaurants. He has picked up enough cooking tips to make anyone into a master chef ... needless to say that he is still trying. When not writing food columns, he can be found squinting in the dark (taking notes for play and movie reviews), going deaf at rock concerts, looking after his two daughters in the afternoons, or watching the Kingston Frontenac games with his son on Fridays. He has been a reporter at the Whig-Standard since 1973, during which time he has covered hockey, football, basketball, horse racing, stock car racing, consumer issues, life styles, movies, plays, books, music, art and records. As with the food column, he professes to be expert in none ... merely an enthusiast.*

Newspapers in 1853

Excerpts from Life in the Clearings Versus the Bush *by Susanna Moodie, 1853.*

"*The Canadian people are more practical than imaginative. Romantic tales and poetry would meet with less favour in their eyes than a good political article from their newspapers ... The standard literature of Canada must be looked for in her newspapers ... A Canadian newspaper is a strange* mélange *of politics, religion, abuse, and general information ... There is no restraint upon the freedom of the press in Canada. Men speak their thoughts boldly and freely. Ay, and print them too, and often run mad in the exuberance of their liberty, if you may judge of their sanity by the intemperate language used in these local journals.*"

11

Raised Turkey Pie

Presented by Paul Fortier,
Old Fort Henry, Kingston, and The Stockade Barracks, Prescott

Ingredients:

pastry crust	turkey, boiled
boiled eggs, sliced	mushrooms, sautéed
onions, sliced	savory to taste
pepper to taste	egg wash

Method:

Begin by rolling out a regular pastry crust in a rectangular shape. De-bone a boiled turkey and break up the meat in large pieces along the grain. Place the pieces of turkey in a tight roll along the center of the pastry crust. Fill in any open spaces with slices of boiled egg, sautéed mushrooms and sliced onions. Sprinkle the turkey liberally with savory and pepper. Do not salt.

Enclose the roll tightly but neatly with the pastry crust. Remember to close the ends. Brush the pastry with an egg wash. Bake for approximately 1 hour in a moderate oven. For service, slice portions about 1 1/2" thick and sprinkle with gravy or the sauce for fowl which appears on the next page.

Paul Fortier is the proprietor of The Stockade Barracks *which operates the food concession at Kingston's Fort Henry and Prescott's Stockade Barracks. His unique business offers a Barracks Banquet which is a historical dining experience offered at Fort Henry in Kingston and at the Stockade Barracks in Prescott.*

The banquet combines a historical environment with good food, high quality service and anecdotes about 19th century military experiences along the upper St. Lawrence River. The dinners and presentation have been developed after extensive research to offer guests an accurate and entertaining dining experience. Diners are treated as guests of the officers' messes at Fort Henry in Kingston during the 1860's and in Prescott during the War of 1812. Service is provided by appropriately costumed soldier-servants.

Turkey past & present

In the early 19th century, it was typical for inhabitants along the upper St. Lawrence River to bake various meats and fowl in pastry.

Turkey, which was — and is — native to North America, was domesticated in Europe and had become popular due to its size and fleshy carcass. One senior officer in the Kingston garrison during the War of 1812 was a notorious turkey gourmand. He fed his turkeys separately on wheat, barley or oats to differentiate the taste.

For years, a wild turkey population has existed on Hill Island in the vicinity of the 1,000 Islands International Bridge. These 'wild' birds supplement their diets with handouts from property owners.

Sauce for Fowl

Presented by Paul Fortier,
Old Fort Henry, Kingston, and The Stockade Barracks, Prescott

Ingredients:

about 1 3/4 oz of port	1/2 tsp of mushroom catsup*
1/4 tsp of cayenne pepper	2 anchovies
3 chopped shallots	juice of 1 lemon

*In the 19th century, mushroom catsup was prepared by extracting the liquor from mushrooms and adding salt, cayenne pepper, allspice, ginger and mace. This mixture was reduced by 1/2 and a few drops of brandy were added.

Method:

Mix the ingredients together and liquify. Reduce the mixture over a low heat to a preferred consistency. The sauce may be served warm or cold. It is an ideal companion for the Raised Turkey Pie recipe which appears on the previous page.

This recipe came from a mid-19th century manuscript cook book that belonged to Louisa Kingsmill, wife of a captain of the Royal Canadian Rifle Regiment who died at Fort Wellington in Prescott in 1853. The recipe was apparently passed on to Mrs. Kingsmill by Captain Talbot, 43rd Regiment of Foot.

Paul Fortier is the proprietor of The Stockade Barracks *which offers its guests the unique chance to dine in a 19th century British officers' mess. For reservations at Old Fort Henry in Kingston, call 530-2550. For reservations at The Stockade Barracks in Prescott call 925-4894.*

Ladies are essential!

Excerpts from Cornhill Magazine, *1862.*

"*Let the reader fancy himself at the top of Fort Henry, the day fine and frosty, his hair and whiskers white, as with a respectable old age, and each point of his moustache the base of an incipient iceberg ... He and his companions are provided with taboggins (sic), and half-a-dozen ladies are of the party, for in Canada ladies are essential accompaniments of merry-making both indoors and out ... A gentleman kneels down at the first taboggin (sic); holds it carefully to prevent a false start; tucks in the lateral superfluities of dress belonging to the lady who has seated herself in the prow of his ship ... cautiously seats himself on the floor behind her, ... a friendly shove and they are off! ... half the fun is in the amusing accidents of less skillful practitioners ... and in obedience to the laws of gravity – though hardly with a grave demeanour – the pilot and his companion roll down the remainder of the hill, without their taboggin (sic).*"

Lighting the way

The inaccurately named 1,000 Islands number 1,865 and there are thousands more rocky shoals. Night time navigation was, and is, fraught with peril yet steamers proliferated in the latter 19th century. Especially popular were night time searchlight excursions.

Lighthouses were erected by the mid 1850's and their beacons burned sperm whale oil. Sadly, this was based on the assumption that sperm whale reproduction rates might keep pace with their slaughter. They didn't; lighthouse keepers switched to kerosene in the late 1850's. Lamps were lighted at sunset and extinguished at sunup. Light reflectors were polished daily.

Automatic beacons ended many lighthouse keepers' careers early in this century and somewhere, a sperm whale is smiling.

Avocados Prawn

Presented by Beba Poole, 1,000 Islands Parkway

Ingredients:

2 cups of small prawns   2 avocados
shredded lettuce   1 lemon

Ingredients for the Sauce:

1/4 cup of ketchup   1/2 cup of mayonnaise
dash of Worcestershire sauce   squeeze of lemon
dash of Tabasco sauce

Method:

Chill the avocados. Peel the defrosted prawns and de-vein.

Blend the ketchup, mayonnaise, Worcestershire sauce, a dash of Tabasco and lemon juice in a small bowl and add the prawns, blending them gently. Cover and chill for at least one hour.

Halve the chilled avocados and remove the seeds. This can be difficult; try sticking a sharp pointed knife into the seed and while holding the fruit, gentle pry loose the seed. Place the halved avocados onto beds of lettuce. Spoon some marinated prawns into each half and sprinkle with paprika (optional). Serve with lemon wedges.

Beba Poole is a nurse. In partnership with her husband, Tony, she manages a pair of delightful rental cottages beside their home on the shore of the St. Lawrence River. Beba says this is one of her favorite recipes because of its simplicity and taste.

Boneless Breast of Duckling in Blueberry & Drambuie Sauce

Presented by The River Mill Restaurant, 2 Cataraqui Street, Kingston

Ingredients:

2 deboned duck breasts	1 oz of Drambuie
1 oz of finely chopped shallots	3 oz of blueberries
1 oz of clarified butter*	3 oz of demi-glaze†
1 oz of honey	salt and pepper to taste
fresh ginger to taste	

*Make clarified butter by slowly melting butter in a small pot. Skim the white foam from the surface and strain through a sieve into a small bowl leaving the milky solids behind. Clarified butter will keep for a long time and does not need to be stored in the refrigerator.

†Demi-glaze is a reduced beef stock. Make your own by reducing 8 cups of brown stock, chilled and fat removed, to 4 cups. Cool and freeze for future use.

Method:

To an oven proof pan, add the clarified butter and pan fry the duck breasts until they are golden brown on the skin side. Turn and place in a 400°F oven for 7 minutes until medium rare. Remove the duck breasts from the pan.

Add shallots and blueberries to the pan. Sauté then deglaze the pan with Drambuie. Reduce by half and add demi-glaze. Season to taste and carefully slice the duck breasts before placing then on a serving dish. Serve with grilled zucchini, stuffed tomato, fried potato ball, green beans secured with a carrot slice and garnish with a curled onion.

Chef Gary Appleton submitted this recipe and the full name of this dish is "Boneless Breast of Brome Lake Duckling in a Blueberry and Drambuie Sauce". The River Mill Restaurant is owned and operated by Colin Altimas and Mark Kennedy.

On housekeeping

The following excerpts are taken from The Home Cook Book *compiled by The Ladies of Toronto and Chief Cities and Towns in Canada, 70th edition, 1877. It contains observation on social conventions as well as recipes. We ask the politically correct to forgive us for quoting from it.*

"... so, no matter how talented a woman may be, or how useful in the church or society, if she is an indifferent housekeeper it is fatal to her influence, a foil to her brilliancy and a blemish in her garments."

"... if Mrs. Smith's sitting room is always neat and fresh, it is because she sweeps it with tea leaves, and sponges the carpet with ox gall, and dusts it with a damp cloth, and keeps a door mat on the porch, and sends the boys back every time to use it till they get the habit of keeping clean."

'Pirate' Bill Johnston

Canadian-born William Johnston was imprisoned by Canada for spying during the War of 1812–14. Upon release, and "breathing revenge", he launched a series of "buccaneering excursions ... to commit a series of arson and robberies several of which were attended with murder", wrote British Royal Marine Captain David Ballingall, an 1841 diarist.

Johnston cloaked his crimes in the guise of Canadian independence. His most notorious act was an 1838 attack upon the steam vessel Sir Robert Peel. Johnston, and 20 members of "his infernal gang" dressed as Indians, stormed the ship as it took on firewood at Wellesley Island. They planned to turn their prize into the flagship of their 'navy' but the klutz factor intervened. Ignobly, they were forced to burn the Peel after inextricably grounding her.

Continued on the next page

16

Boneless Stuffed Chicken
Presented by Sandra Wright, Kingston

Ingredients:
   chicken legs, thighs and breasts
   stuffing (create your own or use a store-bought mixture)

Method:
Debone the chicken and rinse thoroughly. Shake off excess water. Remove the skin, if you wish.

Place chicken parts, deboned side up, on your work surface. Spread the stuffing then roll up the chicken. Excess stuffing will fall out the ends of the rolls. Use toothpicks to skewer the rolls together. Coat the chicken with bread crumbs or with a commercial coating product.

Bake 40 minutes in a 350°F oven, or until done. Cooking times will vary because of the thickness of the chicken rolls.

For variety, make a sauce and cover the chicken just before serving.

Sandra Wright operates Executive Secretarial Services in Gananoque, although she lives in Kingston. When not cooking or commuting, she is a demon baseball player.

Beef Curry

Presented by Katherine Warren, Gananoque

Ingredients:

3 lb of boneless chuck roast or stewing beef
2 tbsp of oil
1 medium onion finely chopped
1 or 2 cloves of garlic, minced
1/2 to 3/4 tsp of salt
1 green pepper (optional)
1 1/2 tbsp of curry powder
1/2 cup of seedless raisins
1 medium apple, sliced (optional)
3 1/2 cups of water

Method:

Cut the beef into 1 inch cubes and brown quickly in hot fat. Reduce the heat and add onion, garlic, green pepper and salt. Add curry powder, stirring well. Add raisins, apple and water and cover. Simmer at least 1 hour or until the meat is tender. Cool and store in a covered dish until you are ready to reheat.

This recipe comes from Katherine's mother, the late Margaret Crouch, who was head waitress for 28 years at Gananoque's Golden Apple Restaurant. Katherine remembers picking wild mint along the Bay Road in Gananoque for The Golden Apple's mint jelly. Her father, the late Fred Crouch, used to catch fish — usually pike, for the restaurant. Today, Katherine works at Gananoque's town hall.

Continued from the previous page

Johnston's predations were abetted by "his daughter a good looking girl of eighteen years of age, who watched his boats as sentinel during her father's lawless operations," wrote the gallant Captain Ballingall. "Her services greatly assisted and facilitated all his schemes and conspiracies by obtaining all the information he might require ...".
Spying, it seemed, came naturally to the Johnston family.

Eventually, the Americans were embarrassed by Johnston's activities so they imprisoned him and his daughter, Kate.

"At the expiration of their first week's confinement, the people not only compelled government to release them, but actually voted that a public dinner should be given to this veriest scoundrel whom they upheld as a patriot, and at the dinner presented a silver oar to the ignorant mermaid daughter whom they designated 'Queen of the Isles'," wrote Ballingall.

Johnston ended his days as keeper of the Rock Island Light located near Clayton, NY. To some he was a hero; others called him pirate.

'Home Improvements'

Excerpts from The Home Cook Book *compiled by The Ladies of Toronto and Chief Cities and Towns in Canada, 70th edition, 1877, which contains observation on social conventions as well as recipes.*

" ... Dexterity with tools is very convenient to anyone and I have known accomplished women who would set a pane of glass, put on a door knob, and hang a gate in the best of style. One of the valued contributors to the New York press is a woman who reads Horace in Latin, and Bastiat's political economy, makes point-lace and embroiders beautifully, who at the gold mines with her husband built the chimney to her house, and finished most of the interior with her own hands."

Home Fried Potatoes

Presented by Manse Lane Bed & Breakfast, 465 Stone Street, Gananoque

Ingredients:

4 or 5 medium potatoes	1/2 tsp of minced garlic
1/4 tsp of parsley flakes	1/2 tsp of Montreal steak spice
1/4 tsp of seasoned salt	margarine or butter

Method:

Wash the potatoes and cut them into quarters. Cook in a microwave according to the directions for your oven, or, about 6 minutes on the high setting. Preheat a frying pan on medium heat and melt sufficient margarine or butter to coat the pan. Add the potatoes and sprinkle with the spices. Stir to coat evenly. Continue cooking for another minute or two, stirring occasionally.

The Manse Lane Bed and Breakfast is owned by Jocelyn and George Bounds. Guests are served a full breakfast between 8 and 9:30 a.m. Picnic lunches are available upon request to guests. Manse Lane offers a smoke-free environment.

This large, brick Victoria house was built in the 1870's by a Gananoque industrialist. The building's interior has been renovated extensively while maintaining its Victorian quaintness. One outstanding exterior architectural feature is a large sun room on the south side of the house. The stained glass doors in front were salvaged from a Toronto commercial building of the same period.

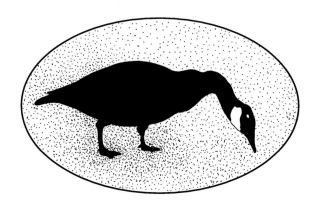

Beef and Potato Cakes
Presented by Beryl Blancher, Mallorytown

Ingredients:

1 cup of cold roast beef, cubed	2 cups of seasoned mashed potatoes
1 egg	bread crumbs
2 tbsp of chopped onion	milk

Method:

Combine the cold roast beef and mashed potatoes, add a beaten egg, moisten with milk and mix. Shape the mixture into balls and flatten each ball to resemble a cake. Roll in bread crumbs then fry a golden brown. These are great for breakfast or tea.

Note on Breading Fried Foods:

Did you ever wonder why many fried foods have a flat taste, even though they may be highly seasoned? The reason is that seasoning has been neglected for the bread crumb coating.

Try mixing the bread crumbs with salt, pepper and, if desired, a drop or two of any other seasoning, before use.

And for frying, or covering the tops of entrées, use bread crumbs instead of cracker crumbs which tend to have a flat taste.

Beryl Blancher was born in Athens and taught elementary school in Northern Ontario and here at home. She worked as a supply teacher for many years then taught grades 7 and 8 at Escott Public School. During the last few years of her career, she acted as school and public librarian in Escott Township. Today, she is retired, lives on a farm with her husband, Phillip, and raises beef cattle.

How many islands?

The 1,865 islands within the 1,000 Islands were formed 12,000 years ago, toward the end of the last ice age. They dot the St. Lawrence River between the Canadian cities of Kingston to the west, and Brockville, 55 miles to the east.

In numerical terms, two-thirds of the islands are Canadian but the total area, or acreage, of the Canadian and American islands is equal. No island is split by the Canada–United States boundary, an arrangement formalized in 1793.

The region was called The Garden of the Great Spirit *by the Indians. Early European visitors, the French, named it* les Milles Isles *which, translated, means the 1,000 Islands.*

Naming the islands

British Royal Navy Captain William Owen is credited with naming many of the 1,000 Islands early in the 19th century. In 1816, naming islands and landmarks was part of his job charting the great inland waterway from the Great Lakes to the Atlantic Ocean.

He divided the islands into groups – The Admiralty Islands, the Lake Fleet Group, the Brock Group and the Navy Fleet. Then he assigned individual island names, each relating to its larger group.

For instance, the Lake Fleet islands are named after British warships as evidenced by their war-like names: Death-dealer, Belabourer, Scorpion and Blood-letter. The Navy Islands are named for distinguished naval officers: Mulcaster, Popham and Cunliffe. Brock Group islands are named for contemporaries of Sir Isaac Brock, who gave his name to the City of Brockville. The Admiralty Islands commemorate British Lords of the Admiralty.

Chicken Florentine

Presented by Main Street's Restaurant, 715 King Street East, Gananoque

Ingredients:

6 boneless, skinless chicken breasts
1 lb of fresh spinach
1/4 tsp of garlic salt
1/4 tbsp of salt and pepper
1 small cooking onion, diced
1 cup of flour

Method:

Steam the fresh spinach until it is cooked. Sauté the diced onion in a little vegetable oil. In a large bowl, combine the salt, pepper, garlic salt, cooked onion and spinach. Pound the chicken breasts but be careful not to make them too thin. Spoon the mixture on top of the pounded chicken breasts then roll the meat. Coat with flour.

Place a large skillet, coated with cooking spray, over medium-high heat until hot. Cook the stuffed chicken breast 1 minute on each side or just until golden brown. Transfer the chicken to a shallow baking pan. Bake at 375°F for 10 to 15 minutes.

Serves 6.

This dish may be served with or without Hollandaise sauce. The recipe for Hollandaise sauce appears on the next page.

This recipe is submitted by Chef Dave Dishart of Main Street's Restaurant at the Country Squire Resort located in Gananoque's east end. Main Street's offers family fare specializing in prime rib, steaks, seafood and pasta dishes. There is a large salad bar and private banquet rooms are available for meetings, parties and weddings.

Hollandaise Sauce

Presented by Main Street's Restaurant, 715 King Street East, Gananoque

Ingredients:

6 egg yolks	1 tbsp of lemon juice
1/4 tsp of salt	1/4 tsp of white pepper
1/2 lb of clarified butter*	2 tbsp of dry white wine

*Make clarified butter by slowly melting butter in a small pot. Skim the white foam from the surface and strain through a sieve into a small bowl leaving the milky solids behind. Clarified butter will keep for a long time and does not need to be stored in the refrigerator.

Method:

In a small saucepan, on low heat, whip the egg yolks and white wine until lightly thickened. With a wire whisk, beat in the clarified butter in small amounts. Add the lemon juice, salt and white pepper. Whisk until this mixture is smooth and creamy.

Psst! Want a deal?

Once, the 1,000 Islands were considered worthless real estate, but a United States' presidential visit in 1872 changed that. The attendant publicity and exposure brought recognition of the 1,000 Islands as an international playground ... on the American side of the St. Lawrence River.

Sales of Canadian islands lagged; only 56 islands had been sold by 1891. Canada published The Thousand Islands For Sale booklet in 1894 and promptly sold 186 islands earning $32,110.

Municipal councils at Brockville and Gananoque petitioned the federal government to keep nearby islands as municipal lands. But the public supported island development because jobs followed for island caretakers and fishing guides.

The average 1894 price per acre was $127. The average 1995 price per acre is $40,000 to $50,000 for undeveloped island property.

Hearts of Oak'?

England's 19th century wood requirements for her navy established Garden Island, near Kingston, as a major transshipment point. Here, oak and pine, harvested throughout the Great Lakes Basin, were assembled into gigantic timber rafts. These were floated down river to Quebec City, broken up and the timber was shipped to England.

Oak was used for naval vessel hulls, the pine for masts and spars. Timbers designated for the navy were marked with a broad arrow symbol. But sometimes the rafts broke up. "Received from Colonel Stone nine pounds – sixteen shillings and four pence – in full for Prize Money – due me – on account of pine spars taken from the American Shore."

The receipt, dated 8 July, 1813, was discovered in the papers of Colonel Joel Stone, Gananoque's founder and official representative of colonial authority.

Chicken Tikka

Presented by Curry Village, 169-A Princess Street, Kingston

Ingredients:

4 boneless chicken breasts
1/2 tsp of cumin
1/2 tsp of garlic
dash of black pepper
1/4 cup of plain yogurt

fresh lime (or lime cordial)
1/2 tsp of turmeric
1/2 tsp of ginger
dash of salt

Method:

Cut the raw chicken into cubes. Sprinkle with 1/2 freshly squeezed lime, or you may use lime cordial. Add cumin, turmeric, garlic, ginger, salt and pepper and place mixture in 1/4 cup of plain yogurt and stir. Adjust spices to taste. Cover and marinate in the refrigerator for 24 hours.

Remove the chicken from the marinade, which is discarded. Place the chicken cubes on skewers and bake in rotisserie oven or on the barbecue. Serve with basmati rice and salad. Serves 3.

Curry Village uses a clay oven and charcoal which imparts a smoky flavor.

Editors' Note:

Chicken Tikka is fine alone, but with a little effort you can turn it into a truly wonderful meal called Butter Chicken. Please read the next page to learn how.

Curry Village is owned by Dewan Ali Afzal and Abdul Hai Chowdhury. The establishment specializes in cuisine from the Indian sub-continent. This recipe was supplied by chef Thi Le who graciously demonstrated how cuisine crosses language barriers. Curry Village is located on the second floor. The ambiance is definitely East Indian, from the wall hangings to the music.

Butter Chicken

Presented by Curry Village, 169-A Princess Street, Kingston

Ingredients:

Chicken Tikka (see previous page)
1 tbsp of clarified butter*
1/4 tsp of garlic
1/4 tsp of cumin
1/4 tsp of ginger
1/2 cup of evaporated milk
raisins and unsalted peanuts to taste
1/2 cup of yogurt

1 tbsp of vegetable oil
1/2 of a medium onion, chopped
1/4 tsp of turmeric
dash of salt
1 tbsp of unsweetened cocoanut
1 tbsp of sugar
1 tbsp of tomato paste
rose water

*To make clarified butter, slowly melt unsalted butter in a small pot. Skim the white foam from the surface and strain through cheese cloth into a small bowl leaving the milky solids behind. Clarified butter will last a long time and does not need to be refrigerated.

Method:

To a frying pan on high heat add the vegetable oil, clarified butter and onion; stir often. Lower the heat when the onion is cooked and add garlic, ginger, turmeric, cumin, salt, tomato paste, cocoanut, milk and sugar. Add raisins and peanuts to taste. Keep stirring to prevent burning. Let thicken then add Chicken Tikka pieces and stir for 10 minutes then add 2 drops of rose water, remove from heat and set on a bed of basmati rice. Garnish with slivered almonds. Serve with salad.

This can be frozen and reheated.

Editors' Note:

This is a spicy company pleaser and is an excellent recipe for cooks who subscribe to the "pinch of this, dash of that" school.

Gigantic redefined

Nineteenth century timber rafts were among the largest man-made objects of that century. Some exceeded a half-mile in length and contained 165,000 cubic feet of timber.

Their composition was oak and pine, the pine supporting the dense oak. Oak sank when the occasional raft broke up. Today, more than a century later, divers discover an occasional, massive, square hewn oak timber preserved by the cold water.

One entrepreneurial diver recovered and sold just such a timber to an architect who used it as the main beam in a Toronto mansion.

The 1,000 Islands themselves were logged over by the 1850's. Second growth covers them today.

A profitable harvest

Clearing land along the St. Lawrence River began in earnest at the end of the late 18th century. United Empire Loyalists – Americans who preferred the British crown to the fledgling US republic – fled to Canada where they were given free land which had to be cleared.

Barrel staves, planks, square timbers and other wood products were created from this wooden harvest. Potash, which was used to make soap, was an important product. European demand, and the United States Embargo Act of 1807, drove potash prices to $320 per ton.

Many settlers, John B. Webster was typical, earned extra money by selling potash. John and his wife, Fanny, built their home north of Lansdowne in 1874. Some of the harvested wood was burned and the ash boiled to produce potash. Today, their great-grandson, Robert, farms land they cleared.

Eggplant Purée with Yogurt
Presented by Casablanca Gourmet Bed & Breakfast
1245 Highway 2, RR 1, Kingston

Ingredients:

3 eggplant	3 tbsp of olive oil
1 1/4 cups of plain yogurt	1 squeezed lemon*
2 crushed garlic cloves	pinch of salt
2 tbsp of finely chopped, fresh parsley	

*Hint: Warm the lemon before cutting it by soaking it in hot water for a few minutes. Much more juice will come out!

Method:

Grill the eggplant until the skins are black and start to blister and the flesh feels soft and juicy. Rub the skins off under the cold tap, taking care to remove any burnt bits. Gently squeeze out as much of the juice as possible, as it is bitter.

Purée the eggplant in a food processor (the traditional method was to use a mortar and pestle). Add the olive oil gradually. Add in the yogurt, mix well then add in the salt, garlic and lemon juice.

Serve cool, garnished with the chopped parsley.

The Casablanca Gourmet Bed & Breakfast is more than a wonderful place to unwind and relax. It offers gourmet dinner and a wide range of cooking classes (hands-on or demonstrations) by Marcel Bahri, a European-trained professional chef. Marcel and Ruth, your hosts, are bilingual in French and English and speak some German and Spanish as well.

Chili Con Playhouse

Presented by Greg Wanless, Kingston

Ingredients:

1 lb 2 oz of lean ground beef
one 8 oz can of baked beans
one 4 oz can of tomato paste
1 green pepper
2 tbsp of chili powder
1 tbsp of curry powder
salt and pepper

one 8 oz can of red kidney beans
one 8 oz can of tomato sauce
1/2 cup of corn
1 medium cooking onion
2 garlic cloves (pressed)
8 tbsp of sour cream
1 tbsp of butter

Method:

Cut the onion and green pepper into small slices.

Brown the meat and drain off the fat. In a large saucepan, simmer the meat, kidney beans, baked beans, tomato sauce, tomato paste and corn. In a small frying pan, lightly brown the green pepper and garlic in 1/2 tbsp of butter and add to the mixture. Lightly brown the onions and curry powder in 1/2 tbsp of butter and add to the mixture. Simmer for at least one hour. Serve with a large scoop of sour cream in the middle. Serves 4 good sized bowls.

Greg Wanless has been cooking up theatre since 1982, mostly at the Thousand Islands Playhouse in Gananoque. Greg also teaches theatre at Queen's University in Kingston. He says he enjoys making nutritious breakfasts for his energetic children. Jeremy and Marcus, however, say they prefer Fruit Loops.

The Gananoque Canoe and Motor Boat Club has produced some of Canada's best paddlers at the provincial, national and olympic levels. Founded in 1906, the membership built the club house in 1909. The Canoe Club operated from the building until 1982 when a group of business people and theatre patrons founded the Thousand Islands Playhouse and transformed the building into a 336-seat theatre. The Playhouse has earned a reputation for the excellence of its live entertainment during its May to October season. Meanwhile, the Canoe Club constructed a new building on the shore of the Gananoque River. To this day, paddlers are much in evidence on both the St. Lawrence and Gananoque Rivers.

Early river travel

Excerpts from Chambers's Edinburgh Journal, *1847, review of an article concerning an 1841 trip by Sir George Simpson, Governor-in-Chief of the Hudson's Bay Company.*

"From Montreal he embarked on the St. Lawrence in light canoes, with the Earls of Caledon and Mulgrave, who visited the wilds of America to enjoy the amusement of hunting ... 'the most important part of our proceedings – the business of encamping for our brief night ... in less than ten minutes our three lodges would be pitched ... our beds were next laid, consisting of an oil-cloth spread on the bare earth, with three blankets and a pillow, and when occasion demanded, with cloaks and greatcoats ... the more experienced voyageurs, after unloading the canoes, had drawn them on the beach with their bottoms upwards, to inspect, and, if needed, to renovate, the stitching and the gumming ...'."

25

Like ... it's gnarly!

Suppose the artist Picasso and Edison the inventor were charged jointly with designing a tree; probably they would create a pitch pine.

Artistically, it is scraggly, gnarly and assumes wild contortions. Practically, its early nickname was candlewood. Its slivers served to light the way for nocturnal visits to that little shack out back.

Pitch pines grow on dry, open southern exposures on both the islands and the mainshore. Needles grow right from the trunk and are bundled in threes, twisting along their length.

This is one of Canada's rarest trees. Some, located in St. Lawrence Islands National Park, have been aged at 200 years. In fact, the pitch pine is the distinctive logo for the national park. Early settlers used it as a source of charcoal, tar and turpentine.

Garlic Spareribs

Presented by Elizabeth Webster Goddard, formerly of Greenfield

Ingredients:

3 lb of spareribs cut in 2 inch pieces	2 or 3 garlic cloves, chopped
2 tsp of salt	one 10 oz can of consommé
2 tbsp of honey	1/4 cup of soy sauce

Method:

Place the ribs in a large bowl. Mix all other ingredients and pour over ribs. Marinate several hours or overnight in the refrigerator. Bake at 400°F for 30 minutes then for another 30 minutes at 325°F. Serve with rice. Serves 6.

Elizabeth Goddard lives in Edmonton but grew up on a farm in Greenfield, north-east of Lansdowne. Her family can be traced back to the United Empire Loyalists who arrived here in the late 18th and early 19th century.

Guinness Stew

Presented by The Toucan/Kirkpatrick's, 76 Princess Street, Kingston

Ingredients:

2 1/2 to 3 lb of stewing beef

1/2 cup of flour

3 celery stalks

5 or 6 parsnips

1 medium turnip

1/4 tsp of rosemary, 1/4 tsp of thyme

1/2 tsp of black pepper

1 tbsp of oil, 2 tbsp of butter

3 crushed garlic cloves

5 or 6 medium carrots

3 medium onions

5 or 6 medium potatoes

1/4 tsp of oregano, 1/2 tsp of basil

salt to taste

water to cover, approximately 3 pints

1/2 pint of Guinness (drink the other half!)

2 beef bouillon cubes dissolved in 1 cup of hot water

2 tbsp of flour plus 1 cup of water mixed well to use as a thickener

Method:

Cut into 1" pieces the stewing beef, celery, carrots and parsnips. Cut into large, rough pieces the onions, turnip and potatoes. Melt the butter and add the oil in a large, heavy pot. Dredge the beef in flour and add to the pot. Sear on all sides to seal the meat. Add celery, onion and garlic and cook 3 minutes longer. Add all spices except salt and pepper. Add the bouillon and enough water to cover the ingredients. Bring to a boil and immediately lower the heat to a simmer.

Simmer for 3 to 3 1/2 hours then add all vegetables and cook until tender. Add salt and pepper to taste. Thicken with the flour and water mixture; add the Guinness. Adjust seasoning to taste. Serve with Irish soda bread (see next page) or other crusty loaf and, of course, lots of Guinness. Serves 6 to 8.

This recipe was submitted by Betty Redmond, kitchen manager and head chef. The Toucan/-Kirkpatrick's offer pub fare made fresh daily. On tap is your choice of 15 draft beers. The Irish pub atmosphere includes displays of rugby team shirts, live music, outdoor patio, and darts. The owners are: Ian Nicholls, Bruce Clark, Arthur Robinson and Bud Gormley.

A century of suds

Kirkpatrick's and The Toucan are twin Irish pubs at 76 Princess Street, Kingston. This historic building, which predates 1840, has been a continually licensed premises since British Army Sergeant William Richardson opened The Beaver Hotel here in 1871. Sergeant Richardson was stationed at Fort Henry.

A copy of Richardson's pub licence hangs in Kirkpatrick's which is named for the city's first mayor. Thomas Kirkpatrick was born in Dublin, Ireland in 1805 and died at Kingston in 1870. The Toucan takes its name from a Guinness advertisement c. 1789 which featured the big-billed bird.

The ornate wooden columns and engraved mirrors of Kirkpatrick's bar mark it as a reproduction of the Irish Newland's bar design c. 1839.

Climate variations

The St. Lawrence River begins near the 1,000 Islands International Bridge at Ivy Lea. The western portion of the 1,000 Islands lie in Lake Ontario.

The lake has a dramatic impact upon local weather conditions. It moderates temperature and humidity fluctuations because it is such a large body of water.

An excellent way to illustrate this is to compare the average, annual number of frost-free days of Aubrey and Stovin Islands. Aubrey, located south-west of Gananoque, averages 160 frost free days. Stovin, some 30 miles down river, near Brockville, averages 143 frost free days.

Another oddity of the 1,000 Islands weather is that storms tend to pass either north or south of the islands.

Irish Soda Bread
Presented by Elizabeth Leighton, Marble Rock Road

Editors' Note:
What better to accompany the delightful Guinness Stew recipe on the previous page than real Irish soda bread. We offer the following authentic bread recipes obtained from a former resident of the village of Mooncoin in Ireland.

Ingredients:

3 cups of white flour	1 1/2 level tsp of baking soda
1 1/2 tsp of salt	2 tbsp of sugar
1 1/2 cups of buttermilk*	1 tbsp of butter or margarine
1/2 cup of raisins (optional)	

*Substitute sour milk or regular milk with one tsp of cream of tartar added

Method:
Mix all dry ingredients in a mixing bowl. Cut in butter and blend. Add the buttermilk and mix well until the mixture has a fairly soft consistency. Turn this mixture onto a floured board and knead for a few minutes. Form in a circle and place on a floured baking tray. Make a cross on top with a knife. Bake at 350°F for 40 to 45 minutes. Place on a wire rack to cool for at least 4 hours. Place in a plastic bag and wrap in a clean tea towel; store in your bread box.

Editors' Note:
Elizabeth bakes this bread at 450° to 475°F in her propane gas oven. We used an electric oven and found that 350°F is about right.

Elizabeth Leighton has worked in the accounting department of a large pharmaceutical manufacturer. She has owned and operated her own business in partnership with John, her husband. For many years the Leightons operated Peck's Marina (also featured in this book) in the Ivy Lea area. She has retired to become a full-time grandmother to Heather, Holly, Violet, Amanda and Samantha.

Irish Brown Bread

Presented by Elizabeth Leighton, Marble Rock Road

Editors' Note: Here is another of Elizabeth's delightful Irish bread recipes.

Ingredients:

2 cups white flour	1 1/2 cups natural bran*
1 1/2 level tsp baking soda	1 1/2 tsp salt
2 tbsp sugar	1 1/2 cups buttermilk†

*Substitute whole wheat flour

†Substitute sour milk or regular milk with one tsp of cream of tartar added

Method:

Mix all dry ingredients in a mixing bowl. Add the buttermilk but stir it in gradually until the mixture has a fairly soft consistency. Turn this mixture onto a floured board and knead for a few minutes. Form in a circle and place on a floured baking tray. Make a cross on top with a knife.

Bake at 350° for 40 to 45 minutes. Place on a wire rack to cool for at least 4 hours. Place in a plastic bag and wrap in a clean tea towel; store in your bread box.

Editors' Note:

Elizabeth bakes this bread at 450° to 475°F for 40 to 45 minutes in her propane gas oven. We used an electric oven and found that 350°F is about right. Remember, however, no two ovens are the same.

Having retired from the marina business to pursue other interests, John and Elizabeth Leighton now make their home on a large, wooded and rocky piece of typical Thousand Islands terrain on Marble Rock Road.

The Lost Channel

In 1760, the British warship HMS Onondaga *was ambushed near the present day site of the 1,000 Islands International Bridge at Ivy Lea. During the battle,* Onondaga's *captain dispatched a boat to warn other British vessels nearby. Then a second boat was lowered and its crew led the* Onondaga *to safety.*

However, the first boat and its crew disappeared. Two or three years later, a passing bateau crew found a smashed yawl bearing the name Onondaga *at the head of the swift channel between Constance and Georgina Islands. No trace was found of the yawl's crew.*

The mystery earned this body of water the name "The River of the Lost Channel". Today, it is called simply "The Lost Channel".

29

"Send a gunboat!"

Gunboats were unlovely craft, used extensively by the 19th century British Navy. These heavy, wooden vessels ranged from 40 to 60 feet in length and 8 to 16 feet in width. Their shallow draught was perfect for navigation in the 1,000 Islands. Each mounted a single, large cannon at the bow.

Gunboats were sloop, schooner, bugger or lateen rigged, but had no keel so their best points of sailing were away from the wind. They were equipped with oars, or sweeps, for use when sailing was not possible.

The wreckage of a gunboat was raised from Brown's Bay in the late 1960's. Today, that wreck is a permanent exhibit at the Mallorytown Landing base of St. Lawrence Islands National Park. The wreck is believed to be that of HMS Radcliffe which was completed in 1817.

30

Djakarta Chicken
Presented by The Clarence Street Grill, 6 Clarence Street, Kingston

Ingredients:

4 boneless chicken breasts	Saag Sauce†
Korma powder*	Banana Brie‡

*Korma powder: mix together 2 tbsp each of curry powder, Mexican chili powder, ground coriander, garam masala, cumin and turmeric, 1 tsp of mace, 1 pinch of cayenne, 1/2 tsp each of cardammon, nutmeg and cinnamon and 1 1/2 tbsp of powdered chicken base. This has a long shelf life if kept in an air-tight container.

†Saag sauce: sauté in 1 tbsp of butter 2 tbsp of finely chopped red pepper and 2 tbsp of chopped, cooked spinach and 1 tbsp of Korma powder. Remove from the heat and let it cool then add about 8 oz of yogurt.

‡Banana brie: blend together in a food processor 1 ripe banana and 1/2 round of small brie, softened, with the rind removed.

Method:

Mix the Korma powder. Wash and pat dry the chicken breasts. Make the saag sauce and keep it slightly warm. Then make the banana brie mixture.

Coat the chicken breasts with Korma powder and sauté in butter and olive oil until cooked through. Place spoonfuls of saag sauce on warm plates. Place the chicken breasts on top and spoon or pipe banana brie on top of the chicken. Sprinkle with paprika or toasted, sliced almonds. This is great with basmati rice and steamed fresh vegetables.

The Clarence Street Grill is owned by Leslie Leacy and Mark Smith and specializes in nouvelle cuisine. Sunday brunch, lunches and dinners are served. In season, enjoy the view of Kingston's harbor from an outdoor patio. Art posters and plants contribute to a feeling of casual elegance. Prices are reasonable.

Dragon's Breath Chicken

Presented by The Kingston Brewing Company, 34 Clarence Street, Kingston

Ingredients:

2 small frying chickens, about 2 1/2 pounds each
2 bottles of Dragon's Breath Pale Ale

1 small onion	1 tbsp of chopped garlic
2 tsp of dried tarragon leaves	2 tsp of dried oregano leaves
1 1/2 tsp of dried basil leaves	2 1/2 tsp of paprika
1/2 tsp of black pepper	1/2 tsp of crushed chilies

1 tbsp of salt (sea salt if possible)

Method:

Slice the onion. Arrange the chicken halves skin-side down in a roasting pan and lay the onion slices on top. Add the beer (available at local beer stores) to partially cover the chicken. Spread the garlic, herbs, chilies and salt over the chickens; gently stir and baste with beer. Cover the pan and let the mixture marinate overnight.

Heat the oven to 400°F. Bake the chicken in the marinade, covered, for 1 1/2 hours. Remove the cover and turn the chicken and allow to bake for another 15 to 20 minutes. Remove the chicken from the marinade and place on an oven tray. Return to the oven and allow the outside to become crispy (about 10 to 20 minutes).

Pour the marinade into a pot and allow to reduce about two-thirds to make a thick glaze. Drizzle the glaze over the chicken before serving.

The Kingston Brewing Company is Ontario's first authentic brew pub. Located in a restored, 19th century building, it operates The Brew Pub and Restaurant, and creates a variety of delightful brews and wines on site. These include Dragon's Breath Pale Ale, White Tail Cream Ale, Aardvark Dark Ale and Pooh's Brew. The owners are Van-Allen Turner and Richard Gilles.

Church service afloat

Church services used to be held every Sunday in July and August beginning in 1887 at Halfmoon Bay, a crescent-shaped inlet of Bostwick Island.

Worshippers came by boat and remained in their craft during services. Boats were tied to a metal rod attached to towering rocky cliffs which surround the bay. The pulpit is a granite block located just above water level, at the bay's back end.

Each week, a different denomination from Gananoque conducted the service. The property was deeded to the Town of Gananoque in 1904.

A number of marriages were solemnized over the years at this romantic location.

31

Jamaican Rice and Peas

Presented by Ruth deLisser, Gananoque

Ingredients:

1 cup of dried red kidney beans*	2 tbsp of vegetable oil
1 medium onion	1 fresh hot red pepper
2 cups of cocoanut milk (thin)	1/2 tsp of thyme
salt to taste	freshly ground pepper to taste
2 cups of long grain rice	

*Pigeon peas are used but dried red beans are more commonly the 'peas' of Jamaican rice and peas.

Method:

Chop the onion into small pieces. Clean and chop the red pepper. Place the beans in a heavy, covered casserole or saucepan with enough cold water to cover by 2". Bring to a boil and reduce the heat; cook at a gentle simmer until the beans are tender, adding hot water during cooking if necessary. Drain the beans, measure the liquid, and return both to the saucepan.

Heat the oil in a frying pan and sauté the onion until it is golden. Add to the saucepan the hot pepper, cocoanut milk, thyme, salt and pepper to taste and the rice. Add cold water, if necessary, so the total is 4 cups. Cook, covered, over very low heat for 20 to 30 minutes, or until the rice is tender and all the liquid is absorbed. Serves 6.

If using fresh or canned pigeon peas, simply add with the rice. Do not cook them beforehand. If using dried pigeon peas, cook exactly as the beans, using 1 cup.

Ruth deLisser is a transplanted Jamaican who practises stress management therapy using a hydrosonic table. A session may include reiki, reflexology, therapeutic touch and incorporates aroma therapy. Her techniques are effective: without them, this book would not exist. Ruth shares her home with a gaggle of friendly, four-legged critters.

Ragoût de boulettes

Presented by Yolande LaPointe, Lansdowne

Ingredients:

1 lb of ground pork*	1/2 lb of lean ground beef
1/4 lb of salted lard (optional)	1 small onion cut into pieces
2 tbsp of parsley	1/4 tsp of ginger
1/4 tsp of cinnamon	1/4 tsp of cloves
1/4 tsp of dry mustard	2 slices of bread, diced
1/2 cup of milk	salt and pepper
3 tbsp of shortening	3 cups of water
4 tbsp of flour	1/2 cup of water

*Instead of ground pork, Yolande prefers meat from 2 pork hocks previously boiled and skinned. She grinds the meat and adds it to the beef. She uses the broth from the pork hocks to replace the 3 cups of water mentioned above.

Editors' Note:

This is an authentic French-Canadian recipe. Translated, it is Meatball Stew.

Method:

Ask your favorite butcher to grind the meat together with the lard (optional). Add the onion, parsley, ginger, cinnamon, cloves, mustard and milk-soaked bread. Season and mix then form into small balls.

Fry the meatballs in shortening for a few minutes. Remove and place in a large saucepan adding 3 cups of water. Simmer slowly for 30 minutes. Fry the flour in a frying pan until it is a golden color. Add 1/2 cup of water, stirring constantly. Stir this paste into the stew adding a bit more water to achieve proper consistency.

Yolande LaPointe is the librarian at Front of Leeds and Lansdowne Township Public Library in Lansdowne. Her husband is retired from the Canadian armed forces.

On social observances

The following excerpt is taken from The Home Cook Book *compiled by The Ladies of Toronto and Chief Cities and Towns in Canada, 70th edition, 1877.*

" ... from three to six are proper calling hours, and a visit may be from five minutes to half an hour, never longer, unless with a very intimate friend. A gentleman leaves his umbrella in the hall, but carries hat and cane with him, keeping the former in his left hand, never venturing to lay it on table or rack, unless invited to do so by the lady of the house. Her not doing so is a sign that it is not convenient for her to prolong his call."

A 'spirited' service

Thaddeus Leavitt, author of the History of Leeds and Grenville 1749–1879, *quotes Mr. Purvis of Mallorytown about two 18th century farmers who found the body of a tramp near Jones' Creek.*

A passing gentleman settled their debate about summoning a coroner. Why incur needless bother and expense, he asked, and contributed $2 to the burial costs. After his departure, the farmers discovered $2.50 more in the corpse's pocket. Neighbors were summoned, a coffin manufactured and services speedily concluded.

"The burial rites being over, it was discovered that a balance of $1.50 remained unexpended. The question immediately arose, as to how it should be spent. By universal consent, it was decided to invest it in spirits. A supply was procured in a pail, the entire congregation assisting in disposing of the same – a task which was speedily accomplished."

RJ's Scampi and Linguine
Presented by Rob Janke, Gananoque

Ingredients:

linguine or other pasta for 4
1/4 cup of olive oil
2 or 3 pressed garlic cloves
4 to 6 green onions
flour
lemon
1/4 cup of freshly grated Parmesan cheese
1 leek or 1/3 cup of sliced Spanish onion

unthawed shrimp, 6 per person
4 tbsp of butter or soya margarine
2 or 3 thinly sliced garlic cloves
1/2 cup of white wine
black pepper
Thai spice (optional)

Method:

Cook the linguine. Meanwhile, in a frying pan over medium heat, melt the butter or margarine in olive oil and sauté the leek or sliced Spanish onion and garlic for a couple of minutes. Do not brown.

Rinse the shrimp well, pat dry on paper towel. Sprinkle with Thai spice. Dredge in flour then cook 1 side for 1 minute. Turn and add sliced green onions and a couple of squeezes of lemon juice. Sprinkle with fresh pepper and cook another minute or until warmed. Transfer to a warmed platter.

Turn heat to low and add wine. Increase the heat until the wine begins to boil. Add the drained and rinsed *al dente* linguine to the mixture and toss with Parmesan cheese and black pepper. Season to taste with extra Parmesan. Return the shrimp to the pan and toss for a few seconds. Serve at once.

Serves 4.

Rob Janke is a semi-retired, successful business person and pharmacist so mixing things comes naturally ... especially onions and garlic, which he loves. This delightful dish may be prepared in 15 minutes.

Pork Tenderloin Medallions & Apple Brandy Sauce

Presented by Peck's Marina & Restaurant, 1,000 Islands Parkway

Ingredients:

2 1/2 lb of cleaned pork tenderloin	16 oz of brown sauce
5 oz of seasoned flour (salt & pepper)	3 oz of Calvados (Apple Brandy)
4 oz of butter	4 oz of oil

Method:

Cut the cleaned tenderloin into 2 oz portions. Stand the portions on end and flatten with a meat hammer. Dredge the flattened medallions in the seasoned flour. In a large frying pan, heat the butter and oil to 350°F then carefully lay in the medallions ,frying them until golden brown on each side.

Remove the meat and deglaze the pan with the brandy. Be careful that it does not flame. Stir in the brown sauce and heat thoroughly.

Arrange the medallions in a fan shape at the edge of a plate and spoon the sauce sparingly over them. Serve with baby carrots, brussels sprouts and roast potatoes.

Serves 4.

This recipe is presented by Don and Kate Hunter who operate Peck's Marina and Restaurant. Located on the shore of the St. Lawrence River, this is a delightful place to visit by car or boat. Don is an accomplished chef who specializes in pastries. In the editors' experience, no one, anywhere in the world, cooks a better French fry! The atmosphere here is casual, relaxed and the vista of the river activity and islands is spectacular.

A monument to love

George Boldt, an immigrant whose first job in New York City was in a hotel kitchen, went on to own Philadelphia's Bellevue-Stratford. Later, by agreement with William Waldorf Astor, he managed New York's Waldorf-Astoria.

Boldt's was the archetypal American rags-to-riches immigrant story. He earned fabulous wealth and much of it found its way into the 1,000 Islands economy.

Boldt built a castle on Heart Island, near Alexandria Bay, New York for his beloved wife, Louise. But she died at 42 in 1904 as the castle was nearing completion. Devastated, Boldt ordered work to cease and it is said he never returned to the site. Boldt died in 1916.

Today, the castle is operated as a tourist attraction by the 1,000 Islands Bridge Authority which acquired it in 1977.

35

Life's little luxuries

In the History of Leeds and Grenville 1749–1879, *author Thaddeus Leavitt quotes this story related by Thomas McCrea of the Rideau.*

"The whole of the inhabitants, for miles around, had gathered to raise a log house ... On the third day, after the last log had been placed in position, a council was held, and, after due deliberation and much discussion, it was decided that the settlement had so far advanced in civilization that some of the luxuries of life should be procured ... It was decided by the council that I should take one and a-half bushels of wheat, carry it from the site of Merrickville to Brockville, exchange it for one dozen bowls, one dozen iron spoons, the balance to be expended in groceries ...

Continued on the next page

Rack of Lamb à la Moutarde
Presented by The General Wolfe Hotel, Wolfe Island

Ingredients:

rack of lamb, 6 ribs per portion	salt
Spanish paprika	ground black pepper
Dijon mustard	honey
coarsely chopped pistachio nuts	

Note:

The rack of lamb should be accompanied by the tarragon sauce recipe on the following page.

Method:

Prepare the rack of lamb by trimming off the back bone and cutting the top between individual cutlets, but leave in one piece. Save the trimmings for stock, except for excess fat. Season the meat with a mixture of two parts salt, one part Spanish paprika and one part ground black pepper.

Broil the rack to your liking then anoint it with dijon mustard and honey, cast in coarsely chopped pistachio nuts and briefly broil again to form a crust.

Cut all the way between the ribs to separate individual cutlets and serve them on top of Tarragon sauce with your favorite vegetables and potatoes.

Miro and Hana Zborovsky are your hosts at this 135 year old hotel which is famous for its award-winning gourmet dinners and spectacular view of Kingston's skyline. The 20-minute ferry ride to Wolfe Island will whet your appetite for a spectacular meal.

Tarragon Sauce

Presented by The General Wolfe Hotel, Wolfe Island

Ingredients:

quartered onions

vegetable oil

flour

tomato paste

white wine

whole black pepper

tarragon

several parsley stems

carrots

onion slices

crushed garlic

fresh butter

salt

Note:

This sauce accompanies the rack of lamb recipe on the previous page.

Method:

Place the lamb trimmings onto a baking tray and brown them in a 350°F oven. When brown, transfer them into a cooking pot and add cold water, quartered onion and a few parsley stems. Bring to a boil and simmer for at least one hour adding boiling water as needed. Let cool then skim the fat from the stock.

In another cooking pot start a vegetable roux as follows: heat a small amount of vegetable oil, add slices of onions and carrots, brown lightly. Add flour, a small amount of tomato paste (for color) and stir till golden brown. Add the cool stock, whisk till smooth, add whole black pepper, crushed garlic, salt and simmer for half an hour, stirring frequently. Strain and season to taste.

In a small pot, reduce the tarragon in white wine and add to sauce. Beat some fresh butter into the warm sauce to add sheen, pour under the rack of lamb and enjoy your dinner.

Continued from the previous page

With the bag on my back, I started for Brockville ... During my journey I was buoyed with the thought of the great surprise ... in store for our good wives ...the matter had been kept a profound secret from them ... I arrived at Brockville on the evening of the second day, pretty tired, and the next day I exchanged my wheat for a dozen white bowls with a blue edge and one dozen iron spoons bright as silver, half a pound of cheap tea and the balance in fine combs and little things for the children. Early next morning, with a light heart, and carefully guarding my precious load, I started for home. I arrived in North Augusta in the evening, and when crossing the stream at that place, on a log, the bark gave away and down I fell, some ten feet on the stones below, and horror of horrors, broke every one of my bowls. Never, never in all my life, did I experience such a feeling of utter desolation. How to go home and meet the expectant people, without the bowls, was an ordeal my soul shrank from, but there was no help for it. I spent a sleepless night on my bed of hemlock boughs, and in the morning proceeded on my way with a sad heart. I found a few of the neighbors at my shanty waiting for me, and was greatly relieved when I saw that the loss was endured with christian fortitude."

Farmed since 1831

"Arrived at Lansdowne November 5th, after twenty-one days' travel with a wagon and span of horses, it being the first wagon that ever passed through the one hundred mile woods to Upper Canada."

Those words were inscribed in a Landon family account book and they record the arrival of Oliver Landon in 1787. He was the first Landon in the area and one of the first settlers in the Front of Leeds and Lansdowne Township.

A United Empire Loyalist, Oliver was born in Litchfield, Connecticut. His descendants have farmed here since 1831.

United Empire Loyalists fled the United States after its 1776 revolution. Most came to Canada which still was part of the British Empire, hence the term "loyalist".

Savory Sausage
Presented by Martha Landon, Lansdowne

Ingredients:

10 lb of ground pork   3 tbsp of salt
3 tbsp of pepper   2 tbsp of powdered sage
1 cup of water

Method:

Mix all ingredients together with your hands. More water may be added if the mixture is not sufficiently moist. The mixture may be put in casings or left in bulk, to be made into patties or cooked crumbled for sausage gravy. Store in the refrigerator.

Martha and her husband Byron live on a Lansdowne area dairy farm which has been farmed by the Landon family since 1831. For a delightful recipe and love story, check out Martha's Elderberry Pie recipe on page 99.

Artichokes & Potatoes au Gratin

Presented by Casablanca Gourmet Bed & Breakfast
1245 Highway 2, RR 1 Kingston

Ingredients:

1 pkg of frozen artichoke hearts, defrosted

1/2 of a lemon	1 cup of milk
3 tbsp of unsalted butter	1/2 cup of chopped onion
1/2 tsp of finely minced garlic	2 large baking potatoes
2/3 cup of heavy cream	pinch of salt
pinch of pepper	pinch of crumbled thyme leaves

Method:

Boil 6 cups of salted water in a large pot. Add the half lemon, 1/4 cup of milk and the artichoke hearts, cover and cook for 3 minutes. Drain the artichokes and slice them diagonally into thin slices. Preheat the oven to 350°F. In a small skillet, melt half the butter and gently cook the onion and garlic until soft, but not brown. Spread the remaining butter on the sides and bottom of a shallow baking pan. Place the onion-garlic mixture into the pan.

Peel the potatoes and slice them as thinly as the artichokes. Do NOT rinse the sliced potatoes. Arrange the potato and artichoke slices in overlapping rows in the gratin dish. In a mixing bowl, combine 1/2 cup of heavy cream, the remaining milk, salt, white pepper, thyme. and blend well. Pour this mixture over the vegetables. It is important to cover the vegetables completely. Bake for 1 hour and 15 minutes. Preparation may be halted at this point, if necessary. The dish can be held up to one hour. Set the dish aside uncovered. Fifteen minutes before serving, preheat the broiler. Spoon the remaining cream over the vegetables and put under the broiler until hot and golden brown. Serve immediately.

The Casablanca Gourmet Bed & Breakfast offers gourmet dinner and a wide range of cooking classes by Marcel Bahri, a European-trained, professional chef.

Famous for fishing

The waters of the St. Lawrence River in the 1,000 Islands region contain more than 80 species of fresh water fishes, including the mighty muskellunge.

In fact, the world record muskie, caught here in 1957, tipped the scales at an ounce or two under 70 pounds. Sportsmen from around the world return year after year to try their luck.

Typical was Herman Reubin of Brooklyn, NY, who celebrated his 92nd birthday on August 16th, 1972, by battling a 35-pound, 52-inch muskie and landing it. Mr. Reubin was a guest of The Gananoque Inn which he patronized for 50 summers, always staying in room 220. His guide was 'Muskie Jake' Huntley of Gananoque.

A Victorian in Canada

Excerpts from Cornhill Magazine, 1862, *written by an anonymous Englishman.*

"They (Canadians—ed.) will be found a gay and hospitable people, attached to the Crown of England, and warmly sympathising in all her interests and undertakings. It has been a too prevalent habit here at home (England—ed..) to class the habits and customs of Canadians in the same long category with American peculiarities ... For a long time this ignorance of the first colony of our empire was intelligible enough ... all point to Canada as demanding from the nations of Europe, and especially from ourselves, a due recognition of her political and commercial status among the nations of the world ... Averse as they are to American rule, and superior as they think themselves to the foibles and peculiarities of the 'Yankee', the intercourse between the two countries, public and private, has for many years been one of the closest intimacy."

40

Shrimp Gratinée
Presented by Sandra Wright, Kingston

Ingredients:

shrimp

cheese

1/4 cup of Caesar salad dressing

1/4 cup of zesty Italian dressing

Method:

In a frying pan, combine both salad dressings and shrimp. Heat thoroughly turning the shrimp frequently. Place the shrimp in gratinée dishes and add left over dressings. Cover with grated cheese to taste. Bake or broil in the oven until the cheese melts and starts to bubble. Serve with bread.

Sandra Wright operates Executive Secretarial Services in Gananoque and lives in Kingston. She has a fondness for very large dogs.

Spicy Grandbanks Codcakes

Presented by The Cook not Mad, 110 Clarence Street, Gananoque

Ingredients:

1 tbsp of butter	4 scallions, chopped fine
3 garlic cloves, chopped fine	2 tbsp of all purpose flour
4 tbsp of sweet red peppers chopped	5 oz of 35% cream
2 tsp of honeycup mustard	1 tsp of chopped fresh basil
1 tsp of chopped dill	1 tsp of chopped tarragon
1/8 tsp of cayenne pepper	1 egg yolk
3 tbsp of fresh lemon juice	1 tsp of salt
3 tbsp of mayonnaise	1 1/2 lb of fresh boneless cod
1/2 lb of cooked Matane shrimp	
1 1/2 tbsp of hot banana pepper chopped fine	

Method:

Lightly grill or broil the cod until just cooked through. Set aside and allow to cool.

In a heavy pot 'sweat' the scallions, garlic, and the peppers in the butter for about 5 minutes. Add flour and cook 5 more minutes, stirring frequently. Do not allow the flour to burn. Add cream slowly, stirring to form a thick paste. Cook for another 5 minutes. Set aside and allow to cool. To this mixture, add the mustard, herbs, cayenne, egg yolk, lemon juice, salt and mayonnaise. Mix well.

Add the cod and shrimp to the mixture and combine well while trying to retain the texture of the fish. *Do not over process*, it should *not* be a smooth, uniform mixture. Handling the mixture carefully, form into 2 oz portions and bread using the traditional breading method. Deep fry until well browned and serve immediately.

The Cook not Mad is owned by Michèle Bussières, Mark Bussières and Nicole LaPrairie. It specializes in regional Canadian cuisine and is smoke free. The restaurant is open for dinner between 5:30 and 8:30 p.m. Call for reservations.

The Cook not Mad

Canada's first published cookbook, The Guide of Rational Cookery or the Cook not Mad, was published at Kingston in 1831.

The Cook not Mad Restaurant derives its name from the book title. In the words of co-owner Mark Bussières: "It has that quirky edge to it that we wanted in the name of the restaurant while still being very serious about the food."

The restaurant offers fine dining with a regional Canadian accent. Capitalizing on the area's rich bounty, and its own garden, the Cook not Mad is a refreshing dining alternative.

Changing daily, a fixed price menu dictates variety and freshness and reflects the kitchen's seasonal commitment. The restaurant is located in historic Britton House, built in 1906, now restored.

41

Hard time in 1836

Excerpts from Rules and Regulations of Kingston Penitentiary in 1836 concerning the duty of convicts.

"Convicts are to yield perfect obedience and submission to their keepers. They are to labor diligently and preserve unbroken silence. They must not exchange a word with one another under any pretence whatever, nor communicate with one another, nor with any one else, by writing. They must not exchange looks, wink, laugh, nod, or gesticulate to each other, nor shall they make use of any signs ... They are not to gaze at visitors when passing through the prison, nor sing, dance, whistle, run, jump, nor do any thing which may have the slightest tendency to disturb the harmony ... They must not carelessly or wilfully injure their work, tools, wearing apparel, bedding, or any other thing belonging to or about the Prison, nor execute their work badly ... For willful violation of any of these duties, corporal punishment will be instantly inflicted."

Spicy Vegetable Pasta
Presented by The River Mill Restaurant, 2 Cataraqui Street, Kingston

Ingredients:

2 1/2 oz of extra virgin olive oil   1 clove of garlic, chopped
1/2 Spanish onion, diced   1/2 carrot cut Julienne
1/2 celery stick cut Julienne   3 chopped tomatoes
1 tbsp of curry powder   1/2 fresh dried red chili
handful of quartered mushrooms   salt, pepper and sugar to taste
10 green beans, trimmed and cut in half
2 tbsp of chopped, fresh parsley and coriander
2 portion size of black pepper spaghetti

Method:

Sauté onions, garlic, carrots, celery in olive oil for 2 minutes. Then add remaining vegetables and spices. Cook for 3 minutes. Cook the spaghetti separately; add it to the pan and toss gently.

Serves 2.

The River Mill Restaurant is owned and operated by Colin Altimas and Mark Kennedy. It is located in the historic Woolen Mill building and overlooks Kingston's inner harbor. The chef is Gary Appleton.

Stifado (Greek Stew)

Presented by Dolly Richardson, Brockville

Ingredients:

3 lb of lean beef stew meat	freshly ground black pepper
salt to taste	1/4 cup of butter
1 1/2 lb of peeled small onions	6 oz of tomato paste
1/2 cup of red table wine	1 oz of red wine vinegar
1 tbsp of brown sugar	1 mashed clove of garlic
1 bay leaf	1 small cinnamon stick
1/2 tsp of whole cloves	1/4 cup of currants

Method:

Cut the meat into 1 1/2" cubes and season with salt and pepper. Melt the butter in a large, heavy kettle with a cover. Add the meat and coat with butter but do not brown. Arrange whole onions over the meat.

Mix 1/2 cup of water and the tomato paste, wine, vinegar, sugar, garlic and bay leaf and pour over the meat and onions. Add the remaining ingredients and bring to a boil. Cover and reduce heat to a simmer, do not stir, for 2 1/2 hours or until the meat is tender.

When serving, stir the sauce gently to blend. Serve with baked acorn squash and a tossed salad.

This can be frozen. Serves 6 to 8.

Dolly has a well deserved reputation as an excellent cook in Brockville. She has been married for 48 years to a World War II veteran, is the mother of two and grandmother of four and, in her own words: "Could anyone ask for more?" Her hobby is rug hooking.

A long winter haul

Ralph Smith of Lansdowne remembers his father drawing hay to Brockville in winter, about 1919. Departure time was 4 a.m. and by daylight he had reached Long Beach, on the city's outskirts. The trip occupied four hours, each way.

Smith Senior delivered his hay to city livery stables and by the time he unloaded and returned to Lansdowne, it was 4 or 5 p.m. Just in time to milk the cows.

Ralph recalls when most travel was by horse and buggy. A good horse in harness could sustain a speed of 20 m.p.h. and cover a great deal of ground, depending upon its breed. While some used their plow horses, others, who enjoyed speed, used retired race horses.

Buggies were decked out with bells and Ralph remembers that he could tell who was coming up the road by the tones of their buggy bells.

43

A true fish story

Gananoque Lake fishing guides pioneered effective conservation techniques more than 60 years before they became popular.

Occasionally, guides were confronted with greedy clients who would, if permitted, catch more than could be eaten. Now these guides realized their fishery was finite and must be protected. After all, fishing was their future.

The situation called for discretion; no one wanted to offend a good client. So the guide would suggest another location, where he knew no fish would bite, while predicting an even greater catch to the client.

This prevented over-fishing. And clients could have no complaints because they had already caught their limits.

Stuffed Sole

Presented by The Glen House Resort, 1,000 Islands Parkway

Ingredients:

four 6 oz sole fillets	2 cups of cream cheese
4 shrimp	1/2 cup of shredded cheddar cheese
garlic to taste	

2 cups of (cooked) crab meat or imitation crab meat

1/2 cup each of diced green pepper, red pepper, celery, mushrooms and green onion

Method:

Mix the cream cheese, crab meat, diced vegetables and garlic together. Put 1/4 of the stuffing in each fillet of sole and roll up. Put shrimp on top and sprinkle with cheese. Place on a pan and bake at 376°F for about 10 minutes.

The Glen House Resort has been operated by the Seal family since 1963. Located on the banks of the St. Lawrence River, The Glen House is in the heart of the 1,000 Islands. This recipe was supplied by chef Jackie McNeil. And the answer is "yes" to those sharp-eyed readers who wonder if The Glen House is owned by the same Seal family which owns and operates the Blinkbonnie in Gananoque.

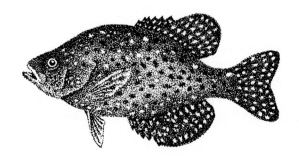

Swedish Pickled Shrimp

's Surf and Turf Store, Barriefield

hrimp	1/2 cup of celery tops
:e	1 tbsp of salt
	8 bay leaves
	3/4 cup of white vinegar
	2 1/2 tsp of celery seed
	3 drops of Tabasco sauce

ater and add celery tops, pickling spices and 1
5 minutes. Do not boil! Drain then peel the
allow baking dish, layer shrimp, onion and bay
ingredients and pour over the shrimp. Cover,
ly spooning the marinade over the shrimp.

glass of chilled, white wine. Serves 6.

ell's Surf and Turf Store in Barriefield Village. He has an
early all of the 200 or so items of fresh fish and seafood
nples and recipes for the asking. For a special treat, stop
hips to go. Or, perhaps you want to add fish to your diet,
ts including salmon, trout, pickerel, sole and haddock
, mussels, crabmeat and more. Mike also sells seafood to
Kingston area.

From:

Dove Cottage Press
160 Georgiana Street
Gananoque ON K7G 1M7
Canada

Gone but not forgotten

Mike Mundell's Surf and Turf Store is located at a Barriefield plaza that once was the site of Smart's Fishery. The proprietor, Sprig Pearson, was a fish monger who trafficked in freshwater perch, pike, sunfish, rock bass, catfish and eels.

Mike recalls: "Sprig could be, well ... crusty, but I always got along well with him. I remember once I called to ask about some fish. He answered in a gruff voice: 'Smart's Fishery,' to which I jokingly replied, 'Excuse me sir, but I am calling from a duck blind on Wolfe Island and ...'"

Mike was interrupted with, "#~!¥§≠µ§ ¢≠#$*!!!!!!!!!!!!"*

"I said, 'Sprig, I could have been someone important calling!' to which he replied 'I don't care if you are the King of England!' There was only one Sprig Pearson and he has gone to meet his maker and I miss him. He was a real part of Barriefield's history."

45

Appearances deceive

Excerpts from Cornhill Magazine, 1862.

"We will now turn our attention to the defences already existing in Canada ... At Kingston there is more show of defence. Moats, battlements, and escarpments, are there, though we are told that they are but a semblance. Fort Henry, the resort of many a merry taboggining (sic) party, to the unsophisticated civilian shows an imposing front: official reporters, however, set it down as nil*. Martello towers, too, dot the circumference of the harbour, and with an Armstrong gun planted on the platform at the top of them, seem of undeniable utility in protecting the entrance of the St. Lawrence, and the Rideau Canal to Ottawa."*

46

Warm Steak & Pepper Salad
Presented by The Wellington, 207 Wellington Street, Kingston

Ingredients for the Oriental Dressing:

1/2 cup of red wine vinegar	1/2 cup of soy sauce
4 tbsp of minced garlic	2 cups of olive oil
2" of fresh peeled, chopped ginger root	

Other Ingredients:

6 oz New York sirloin	iceberg & romaine lettuce, mixed
broccoli	red cabbage, chopped fine
cauliflower	chopped carrot
red peppers cut into long strips	other vegetables as desired

Method:

In a food processor, mix vinegar, soy sauce, garlic, ginger root and olive oil to create the dressing.

On a serving platter, arrange lettuce, carrot, broccoli, cauliflower, red cabbage or other fresh, raw vegetables. Clean the peppers and cut into long strips. Grill both peppers and the steak to taste then cut the steak into long strips and arrange both peppers and steak in a sunburst pattern on top of the salad. Add dressing to taste.

This unique and tasty meal also lends itself to the barbecue.

The Wellington is a pub in the Irish tradition down to dark wood paneling and traditional bar design. Exposed limestone testifies to the heritage nature of the building which once housed a bakery. Today, it offers patrons a choice of tables or cozy booths, a fireplace, darts and pub 'fayre'. Ten beers are on draft; five of them are imported. Manager Peter Schwarz says The Wellington offers some of the finest live music in the city. Monday is blues night; Thursday, jazz; Friday and Saturday nights, Celtic music including performances by Gerry O'Kane, one of the pub's owners; Sunday afternoons feature a live jazz jam and Sunday nights, the Kingston Folk Club. Entertainers range from internationally known to the best of local artists.

Comments:

Turkey Burgers

Presented by Windmills Café, 184 Princess Street, Kingston

Ingredients:

1 1/2 cups of white bread crumbs	3 eggs
1/4 cup of stripped thyme leaves	1/4 cup of dijon mustard
2 tbsp of mustard seeds	3/4 cup of minced onion
2 tbsp of crushed, black pepper	1 to 2 tsp of salt
1 tbsp of paprika	toasted bagels
dijonaisse	lettuce
tomato slices	red onion slices
corn relish (ramekin)	10 lb of ground turkey

Method:

Combine the bread crumbs, eggs, thyme, dijon mustard, mustard seeds, onion, pepper, salt, paprika, turkey and mix well. Make into patties and store layered in the fridge.

Grill burgers for 3 minutes on each side and assemble beginning with the toasted bottom of the bun. Add the dijonaisse, lettuce leaf, turkey burger, 2 tomato slices, red onion slices and cap the burger with the toasted top bun. Serve with ramekin of corn relish and a green salad. Makes 32 burger patties.

Windmills Café, in the heart of downtown, is Kingston's popular rendezvous which offers gourmet breakfasts, imaginative and intercontinental cuisine for both lunch and dinner in a casual, colorful atmosphere. Original paintings decorate the walls. There is an amazing array of desserts made on the premises. Further, Windmills Café is a full service caterer which offers fresh, gourmet foods and baked goods.

All that we needed

The land, and your own hard work, provided almost everything necessary for life, earlier this century. Pat Lackie and Lilian Griffin, Lansdowne sisters-in-law, recall that some of the menfolk worked as fishing guides.

During The Depression, Lilian remembers her husband, Bill, earning $4 a day for guiding. Trapping too contributed as much as $4 or $5 for each muskrat pelt.

Pat remembers the family orchard produced a cash crop. In season, she picked berries and sold them. And there was the Lyndhurst Turkey Fair where families, like hers, sold turkeys, some 70 years ago.

Back then, pork and pickles were salted and ham was smoked with store-bought 'liquid smoke' to cure it. Bread, butter, soap, vinegar and even ice cream were made at home. Fish and game supplemented the diet.

Ballroom warriors

Excerpt from Cornhill Magazine, 1862.

"The Canadian Militia is celebrated in history ... By law, every male adult under a certain age is enrolled on the list of the militia. This has been divided into two branches, 'the active' and 'the sedentary' ... An undue feeling of security, and the universal occupation consequent on business and progress in a new country, have led to a fearful glut of the 'sedentary' commodity, and, notwithstanding the efforts here and there of a few zealots, with leisure and ability to encourage military exercises, the regiments of militia, with a few notable exceptions, have given proof of their existence rather on paper than in the field ... There are few houses in Canada where a militia uniform does not occupy a corner of the wardrobe — to grace the exterior of its owner on grand occasions; more generally, though, under the glittering light of ballroom chandeliers, than under the open canopy of the sky."

48

Wiener Schnitzel

Presented by Amadeus Café, 170 Princess Street, Kingston

Ingredients:

four 6 to 8 oz schnitzels*	2 or 3 eggs
milk	salt
flour	bread crumbs (not too fine)
oil	butter

*If you do not have a European butcher to cut proper schnitzels, use butterfly porkchops. The end of the loin makes a tastier schnitzel.

Method:

Pound the schnitzels with a mallet to 1/4" or less in thickness. Make small cuts in the edge of the meat to prevent curling. Salt both sides, flour both sides and shake off the excess flour. Dip in the egg wash (egg and milk) then dip in the bread crumbs. Do not press too hard. Immediately place them into 1/2" of hot fat (vegetable oil, not olive oil, and butter mixture) in the frying pan.

The oil has more tolerance for heat than butter, thus the butter browns and the oil cooks the schnitzel. If you are making larger quantities, change the fat frequently to keep a consistent, golden color. Keep warm in the oven with layers of paper towel between each schnitzel. Serve with lemon wedges and tossed or potato salad, rice or home fries (see next page). Serves 4.

Amadeus Café is owned by Peter and Inge Breitwiser who are joined by their son, Brian, and his wife Sherri. Peter, who also is the chef, was trained in Linz, Austria, and has cooked all his life. The Breitwisers designed their restaurant and completed necessary renovations themselves. The result is delightful old world charm right down to the calligraphy on the menu. Off-white stucco walls and dark green wainscotting, comfortable caned chairs — all combine to produce an elegant yet casual atmosphere. The menu features German-Austrian cuisine and fresh food selected daily by family members.

Potato Salad — Vienna Style
Presented by Amadeus Café, 170 Princess Street, Kingston

Ingredients:

8 mid-sized boiled potatoes	1 medium cooking onion
salt	pepper
oil	vinegar
1/2 cup of chicken or beef stock, heated	

Method:

Place the finely chopped onion in a mixing bowl. Cut the potatoes and place on the onions while still warm. Add salt, pepper, vinegar and oil to taste. Now, add the hot stock, mix with your hands and serve warm.

Amadeus Café, named after composer Wolfgang Amadeus Mozart, offers a variety of home-made soups and sauces using natural herbs and spices without additives or preservatives. The menu includes such German-Austrian delights as rouladen, goulash, schnitzel and various sausage dishes. Original desserts include Crêpe Mozart Apples flambé.

New in 1995 is an outdoor Bavarian beer garden with seating for 50 to 60 people. This terraced courtyard is surrounded by walls which make this an inviting place to indulge in one of the additive-free draft beers served here. Finger foods are available or you may choose from the regular menu.

Winter in Kingston

Excerpts from Cornhill Magazine, 1862.

"And now for a word or two about the pastimes and amusements of a Canadian winter ... Snow roads are nothing like the 'high hard road' of summer, and properly roughed and shod, horses take no harm even on ice. At Kingston, it is a common thing to see trotting races, in light American sleigh-sulkies, over the ice between the town and Garden Island; and the ordinary winter passage of travellers between Kingston and New York is in a stage, which, for several months, is driven across the twelve miles of ice between the former place and Cape Vincent. Other resources for the energetic are — meetings of the snowshoe club, the curling sheds, skating rinks, or the more obstreperous pastime of taboggining (sic)."

A 19th century killer

Early settlers faced many challenges but few as deadly as a malaria epidemic. The following account appears in Thaddeus Leavitt's History of Leeds and Grenville 1749–1879 *and describes what happened at Gananoque.*

"For many years the place was very unhealthy, fever and ague prevailing in consequence of the swamps surrounding the settlement. In 1826–27, the malaria fever nearly decimated (sic) the settlement. Six out of the McDonald household died. Business was suspended, and most of those who were able left the place."

The malarial scourge also ravaged the ranks of those building the Rideau Canal, begun in 1826, which links Canada's first capital city, Kingston, with the present capital, Ottawa.

Bottle O' Wine Stew

Jan Gravelle, Gananoque

Ingredients:

2 lb of stewing beef	1 small sliced Spanish onion
6 carrots	1/2 bunch of celery
4 medium potatoes	1 1/2 cups of flour
2 tbsp of vegetable shortening	1 bottle of Piat d'Or red wine

1/2 tsp each of salt, basil, celery salt, ginger, garlic powder, cinnamon, and freshly ground black pepper

Method:

Cut the stewing beef into bite-sized pieces; pare the vegetables then slice the carrots and onion, cut the potatoes into chunky cubes and chop the celery. Parboil the vegetables.

Place flour and seasonings in a plastic bag; add beef a handful at a time and shake to coat evenly. In a frying pan, brown the beef in the vegetable shortening. Cook for 10 minutes at high in a pressure cooker with 1 tbsp plus 1/4 cup of water, or, simmer in 1/2 cup of wine and water, just enough to cover the meat, for 2 hours. Then drain off the liquid into a smaller pot.

Thicken the liquid with leftover seasoned flour and a little water, if it is not already thick. Add 1/2 cup of wine. Return the gravy to the meat pot and add the parboiled vegetables. Leave on minimum heat for at least 1 hour to let the flavors blend. Just before serving, taste ... add a little wine. Serve with fresh French bread and the rest of the wine. Should serve four but you may need more wine!

Jan Gravelle shares life with husband, Doug, a pair of Sheltie dogs and a cat. Her recipe is Scottish but has been "doctored" by four generations of her family. Jan says: "Somewhere between my grandmother and me, the Scotch whiskey became red wine ... about the same time the garlic powder was introduced."

Garlic Bread
Presented by Mayone Kelly, Marble Rock Road

Editors' Note:

This is the best garlic bread we have ever had; it has a light, even texture and is easy to make. It is a 'must' for garlic lovers.

Ingredients:

1 pkg of dry yeast	1/4 cup of warm water
1 cup of cottage cheese	1 1/2 tbsp of garlic spread*
2 tsp of salt	1/4 tsp of baking soda
2 tbsp of sugar	1 egg
1 tbsp of melted butter	2 1/4 cups of flour (approximately)

*To make garlic spread, place the desired amount of cleaned garlic cloves in a blender and turn to high setting while adding olive oil gradually until the garlic resembles a butter-like paste. Make lots and freeze the left-over paste in a small container or ice cube tray for use in pasta dishes, stews or more bread.

Method:

Dissolve the yeast in the water and set it aside. In a large bowl, combine the cottage cheese, garlic, baking soda, salt, sugar and egg. Stir in the yeast mixture and flour. Knead for 5 to 10 minutes on a floured board. Let this mixture rise in a greased bowl until it has doubled in bulk, about 1 hour. Punch it down, shape, and place in two greased loaf pans (4" by 8") and let rise for 45 minutes. Bake at 350°F for 30 minutes. Remove from the pans and brush with melted butter.

Mayone Kelly née Cross grew up on the family farm in Warburton and can trace her family back to a United Empire Loyalist ancestor. Today, Mayone and husband Wayne, a retired Canadian Armed Forces infantryman and Korean War veteran, share their home with a very large, lovable dog named Max.

Some 'milk run', that

As a girl, Mayone Kelly's morning job was to round up the horse, hitch him to a wagon and haul cans of fresh milk to Warburton's cheese factory, north of Lansdowne. You could count on Mayone not to dawdle ... especially if a particular neighbor was hauling milk at the same time.

"When I could see him coming, he'd speed up," she recalls. "Then I'd try to beat him to the factory ... if Dad had known, he would have killed me!"

On the return trip, Mayone hauled whey which she poured into a trough for livestock to drink. Once, in haste, Mayone clanked two milk cans which startled the horse (undoubtedly feeling his oats for winning the morning race). "Well the horse took off and I went head first into the whey!"

Mayone admits that to this day she draws upon all available horsepower.

Colonial deadbeats?

Excerpts from Chambers's Edinburgh Journal, *1847.*

"The United Kingdom owns upwards of forty dependencies ... The principal colonies ... are Canada, Nova Scotia and New Brunswick ... Taking them altogether, the great question is continually obtruding itself – What is the use of these colonies to Britain – what does she make of them? The answer perhaps is, that they were acquired, and are sustained, at a great cost, for the sake of their trade ... Have they realized our expectations ... are they found to pay? The people of Great Britain are surely concerned in knowing the truth on such a subject ... The colonies are not taxed. They contribute nothing, in a direct manner, to the revenue of the mother country, who defends them with her fleets and armies at her own proper charge."

Yorkshire Pudding
Presented by Caiger's Resort & Fishing Lodge, Rockport

Ingredients:

1 cup of milk	1/2 cup of flour
2 eggs	1/2 tsp of salt

Method:

Beat the flour and milk. Add the eggs separately, beating into the flour and milk mixture.

Take 1/2 cup of drippings from your roast and place in an 8" by 8" pan. Heat the pan in the oven until very hot. Pour the batter immediately into the pan. Bake at 500°F for 10 minutes then lower the heat to 350°F and bake for another 20 to 25 minutes.

This recipe can be doubled, tripled, quadrupled or more.

Caiger's Resort & Fishing Lodge is owned and operated by the Spafford family. Much of the cooking is done by Margaret Spafford who says this recipe for Yorkshire Pudding is very popular and she serves it with prime rib and gravy. The lodge has had a reputation throughout the 1,000 Islands for excellent dining since 1945 when Frank Caiger and his wife, Anne, began with a farmhouse with three bedrooms.

Their daughter, Margaret, married Gordon Spafford, an educator. In 1970 Gordon and Margaret took over the operation and ran it successfully for years. But fire levelled the main lodge and several motel units in 1981. Undaunted, the Spaffords rebuilt while retaining the homey atmosphere. Today, their son Gordon Jr. has joined them in the family business.

Chicken Tarragon Casserole

Presented by Frances Smith, Kingston

Ingredients:

6 boneless, skinless chicken breasts	2 cups of fresh mushrooms
2 cups of chicken stock or bouillon	1 lemon
1 tbsp dry tarragon leaves (or 3 fresh)	black pepper
2 tbsp butter	2 tbsp olive oil

Method:

Cut each chicken breast into 3 pieces and marinate, in the refrigerator, in lemon juice for 2 to 3 hours. Turn 3 or 4 times. Drain and save the marinade.

Gently sauté the chicken in oil and butter for about 6 minutes, turning once; remove to a casserole. In the same pan, gently sauté the mushrooms which have been cut into quarters; remove to the casserole. Sprinkle tarragon herbs over chicken and mushrooms in casserole.

Make the sauce in the same pan by mixing chicken stock with lemon marinade to make 2 cups. Pour it into the frying pan and simmer to reduce to about 1 1/2 cups, add 1/4 cup of sherry if desired. Blend 1 1/2 tbsp flour in a little water and add to the stock, stirring, over medium heat, until slightly thickened. Season with pepper (salt may not be necessary depending upon the chicken stock used).

Spoon sauce over contents of casserole, cover and bake in 350°F oven for 30 minutes. Remove cover and bake 10 minutes more. Parboiled and sliced young carrots add a colorful accent to the casserole. Serve with wild or white cooked rice. Serves 4 to 6; cut quantities by half to serve two.

Frances Smith is an art historian and author. She is curator emeritus of the Agnes Etherington Art Center at Queen's University and author of André Bieler — an Artist's Life and Times and Daniel Fowler, 1810-1894. She also is an accomplished wood carver and has long been associated with the MacLachlan Wood Working Museum.

The cost of Canada

Excerpt from Chambers's Edinburgh Journal, *1837.*

"Our (the British—ed.) *ascendancy in Canada, at this moment, is wholly dependent on the presence of a large military force, occasioning, one way and another, a direct outlay of little less than £1,500,000 a year; and all this heavy expense is incurred without any equivalent advantage, and with a full conviction on the mind of every man of sense in the empire that, at no very distant period, Canada will be independent, or an integral portion of the United States!"*

Editors' Note: It is worth remembering that Canada become a country in 1867, 30 years after the above comment. It has yet, however, to become "an integral portion of the United States". The quotation is attributed to a gentleman named M'Culloch in 'his newly published work'.

Progress with a bang

Mediterranean Tart
Presented by Casablanca Gourmet Bed & Breakfast
1245 Highway 2, RR 1, Kingston

Ingredients for the Pastry:

2 cups of all purpose flour	1 cup of olive oil
1/3 cup of water	1 egg
salt	black pepper

Ingredients for the Filling:

1 small eggplant	2 garlic cloves, finely chopped
2 thinly sliced onions	1/4 cup of olive oil
6 small thinly sliced tomatoes	4 small thinly sliced zucchini
1 tsp of fresh thyme	salt and pepper
2/3 cup of pitted, halved, black olives	

Method:

Blend all pastry ingredients in a food processor with a plastic blade for 2 minutes. Roll the dough into a ball, cover with plastic food wrap and refrigerate for 1 hour.

Cut the eggplant lengthwise and slice each half very thinly. Fry the eggplant, garlic and onions in olive oil over a moderate heat for 15 minutes or until the eggplant softens. Stir in the salt and pepper and most of the thyme. Set this mixture aside and preheat the oven to 425°F.

Roll out the pastry and put into a tart tin with a removable base. Trim the excess pastry from the edges and prick the base with a fork. Spread the eggplant mixture over the base. Arrange the sliced tomatoes and zucchini decoratively over the top. Top off with black olives, sprinkle with remaining thyme and brush with olive oil. Bake for 45 minutes and serve hot or cold.

The Casablanca Gourmet Bed & Breakfast offers gourmet dinner and a wide range of cooking classes by Marcel Bahri, a European-trained professional chef.

Tomato/Cheese Bake

Presented by Frances Smith, Kingston

Ingredients:

6 slices of bacon
3 cups of soft bread crumbs
salt and pepper to taste
2 tbsp of butter

1 chopped medium onion
6 sliced medium tomatoes
2 cups of grated cheese*

*half cheddar, half mozzarella

Method:

Cut the bacon strips into pieces and sauté in a frying pan until they are almost crisp. Set them aside and reserve the fat. Sauté the onions in the same pan and set them aside.

In a large frying pan, melt the butter, add the bread crumbs and heat well, tossing continually with a spatula until the crumbs are crispy.

In a square or oblong baking dish, make two layers of tomato slices, bacon, onion, crumbs and grated cheese, seasoning each layer to taste. The top layer should be composed of tomato slices and grated cheese and a few crumbs.

Parmesan cheese may be used for variety on the top layer.

Bake at 350°F for about 40 minutes.

Frances Smith is an art historian and author. She is curator emeritus of the Agnes Etherington Art Center at Queen's University and author of André Bieler — an Artist's Life and Times *and* Daniel Fowler, 1810-1894. *She also is an accomplished wood carver and has long been associated with the MacLachlan Wood Working Museum.*

St. Lawrence skiffs

Around the 1860s, a remarkable river boat called the St. Lawrence skiff was created. This double ended craft was light, very fast, easily rowed, and could be equipped with sails.

The St. Lawrence skiff was intended as a fishing boat but rapidly became popular with recreational boaters and anyone else whose work or play required river travel.

These skiffs are no longer manufactured commercially although there is the occasional craftsman who will make one to order. And at every antique boat show there are always a variety of restored St. Lawrence skiffs on display.

A profitable prison

Kingston Penitentiary has been a landmark for more than 150 years and convict labor helped to build the massive limestone structure. The following diary entries were made by a visiting British Royal Marines officer in the early 1840's.

"A most remarkable feature of this establishment is that the convicts have been actually made to imprison themselves by the labour of their own hands in the erection of the edifice by blocks which they are compelled to quarry and hew from a strata of horizontal limestone found on the site."

Convicts worked 13 hours a day.

"The great object of this system of imprisonment is the convicts shall be made by labour not only to defray all the expenses of the establishment but realize a profit to the province. The rope walk alone even in the present incomplete state of this edifice lets together with the labor of 15 convicts employed in the manufacture of rope £500 per annum."

Chicken Salad with Curry
Presented by Erik Alstrup, Kingston

Ingredients:

1/2 cup of non-fat yogurt	2 tbsp of lemon juice
1/4 tsp of curry powder	1/4 tsp of pepper
one 8 oz cooked chicken breast	1/4 cup of diced celery
2 tbsp of raisins	1 tbsp of sunflower seeds
lettuce leaves	

Editors Note:

This recipe is presented by a body builder and health club manager who designs exercise routines for one of the editors of this cookbook. And Erik is well equipped to enforce any edict about eating spinach so we gladly and respectfully offer the following nutritional information.

Per serving, this recipe contains 238 calories, 31 grams of protein, 19 grams of carbohydrates and 8 grams of fat.

Method:

Dice the chicken breast. Combine yogurt, lemon juice, curry powder and pepper in a mixing bowl. Add the remaining ingredients, except for the lettuce, and toss.

Arrange the lettuce leaves on salad plates and add the chicken salad. Serves two.

Erik Alstrup is a manager at Gananoque's Country Squire Squash and Health Club. He designs personal training programs for clients and offers nutritional advice to help them achieve fitness goals. Erik eats this high protein, low fat dish frequently when dieting to compete as a body builder, his future occupation.

Cornbread with Leeks and Peppers

Presented by The Cook not Mad, 110 Clarence Street, Gananoque

Ingredients:

3 cups of all-purpose flour	5 tsp of baking powder
2 tbsp of white sugar	2 tsp of salt
1 cup of yellow cornmeal	2 eggs
6 tbsp of olive oil	2 cups of buttermilk
4 oz of chopped leeks	4 oz of diced red peppers
1/2 tsp of nutmeg	

Method:

Sift the flour, baking powder, white sugar, salt and yellow cornmeal together in a stainless steel bowl. In another stainless steel bowl, combine and whisk together the eggs, buttermilk and olive oil.

In a heavy pot, sweat the leeks, peppers and nutmeg until soft. Remove from the pot and set aside to cool.

Wipe a loaf pan generously with an oiled rag and place the empty pan in a convection oven at 450°F until the pan just begins to smoke. Meanwhile, combine the dry ingredients, wet ingredients and leeks and peppers. Mix well by hand but do not overwork.

Immediately place the batter into the smoking pan, place in the oven and reduce the heat to 300°F. Bake for 1 1/4 to 1 1/2 hours or until a skewer inserted in the center of the loaf comes out clean. Yields 1 large loaf or 2 small loaves.

The Cook not Mad is owned by Michèle Bussières, Mark Bussières and Nicole LaPrairie. It specializes in regional Canadian cuisine and is smoke free. The restaurant is open for dinner between 5:30 and 8:30 p.m. Call for reservations.

1860's naval matters

Excerpt from Cornhill Magazine, 1862, written by an anonymous Englishman travelling in Canada. Bear in mind his observations were made some 48 years after the War of 1812–14.

"At the close of the war it was agreed between the high contracting parties that neither power should build or maintain a naval establishment on the lakes. This part of the treaty has been scrupulously observed at all events on the side of the colonists. The wharves and storehouses in Navy Bay, the headquarters of the old marine at Kingston, have long ago sunk into ruin and decay, there is not a vestige left of the old ships forwarded from England in pieces, and, as the story goes, fitted with large immovable water tanks, to float over the freshwater waves of Ontario!"

Old Fort Henry

Serious thought was given to Kingston's defences after the War of 1812–14. It is said that England's Duke of Wellington, the victor at Waterloo, studied maps of Kingston and suggested the construction of fortifications at the present site of Fort Henry. Further, the Iron Duke, as he was called, envisioned a waterway linking Kingston to Ottawa ... that vision became the Rideau Canal.

Construction began in 1826 on Fort Henry. Meanwhile, a military engineer named Colonel John By was charged with building the Rideau Canal. The canal was completed by 1832 while work on the fort lagged because of disagreements about the extent of the fortifications.

The fort's citadel was completed by 1836 and outer defences by 1848. A network of Martello Towers was built to provide interlocking fields of fire.

Feta and Garlic Pâté

Presented by The Chinese Laundry Café, 291 Princess Street, Kingston

Ingredients:

2 minced garlic cloves
6 tbsp of softened butter
6 oz of feta cheese
1 tbsp of chopped, fresh chives*
a pinch of freshly ground pepper

4 minced anchovy fillets
10 oz of cream cheese
1/4 cup of sour cream
a few drops of Tabasco sauce

*green onions may be substituted for the chives

Editors' Note:

You may wish to try this spread on Joan Nicholson's bread; her recipe appears on the next page.

Method:

Combine the ingredients in a food processor until they are very smooth and creamy. Spread on crackers, bread or bagels. This pâté is also terrific in sandwiches. This recipe makes about 2 cups.

The Chinese Laundry Café specializes in desserts made on the spot. It is famous for its cheesecakes and 10 to 12 different, daily selections. Manager Janet Smith says the homemade soups are the best in Kingston. Even the bagels are made on the premises. There is a large selection of teas, both herbal and regular and the café is fully licensed. Only fresh ingredients are used without chemical additives or preserving agents. Most menu items are priced under $8.

For some 40 years, a Chinese laundry operated here, hence the name, Chinese Laundry Café. Contemporary music and original paintings by Mark Graham add to the eclectic, bohemian décor and ambiance. The Chinese Laundry Café is owned by Ann Marie Rousseau.

Joan Nicholson's White Bread

Presented by Joan Nicholson, Lansdowne

Ingredients:

2 cups of milk	1/4 cup of sugar
4 tsp of salt	1/4 cup of shortening
1 cup of water	9 to 10 cups of flour
2 tbsp of fresh, dry yeast	1 cup of lukewarm water
2 tsp of sugar	

Method:

Sprinkle 2 tbsp of fresh, dry yeast over 1 cup of lukewarm water in which 2 tsp of sugar has dissolved. Let stand for 10 minutes then stir briskly with a fork.

Scald the milk with shortening. This may be done in the microwave oven, approximately 4 minutes on the high setting. Pour into a large mixing bowl; add the sugar, salt and water.

When the milk mixture has cooled to lukewarm, add the softened yeast and stir. Beat in approximately 9 to 10 cups of all-purpose or unbleached white flour. Knead the mixture until it is firm and elastic to touch then place in a large, greased bowl. Lightly grease the top, cover and allow the dough to rise in a warm, draft-free place until doubled in bulk. Punch it down and divide into 4.

Knead and shape into loaves and place in 4 greased bread pans. Cover the pans with a cloth until the dough has risen. This should take approximately 1 hour. Bake at 375°F for 30 to 35 minutes until golden brown. When tapped on the bottom, they should sound hollow.

Joan Nicholson née Arlt was born and raised in Creston, BC. Today she lives on a sheep farm with her husband, Henry. They have two children in university. Joan works at the Lansdowne Public Library and, when not baking for pleasure, she reads, writes letters and helps on the family farm.

19th century yeast

The following excerpt is taken from The Home Cook Book *compiled by The Ladies of Toronto and Chief Cities and Towns in Canada, 70th edition, 1877. The book contains observation on social conventions as well as recipes.*

"Grate six good sized potatoes (raw); have ready a gallon of water in which has been well boiled three handfuls of hops; strain through a cloth or sieve, while boiling hot, over the potatoes, stirring until well cooked, or the mixture thickens like starch; add one teacup of sugar, one-half cup of salt; when sufficiently cool, one cup of good yeast. Let it stand until a thick foam rises upon the top. Care must be taken not to bottle too soon, or the bottles may burst. Use one coffee cup of yeast to six loaves of bread. If kept in a cool place this yeast will last a long time, and housekeepers need not fear having sour bread."

Corn Bread

Presented by The Brockville Museum, 5 Henry Street, Brockville

Ingredients:

1 cup of flour	1 cup of cornmeal
2 tbsp of sugar	3 tsp of baking powder
2 eggs	1 cup of milk
1/4 cup of salad oil	

Method:

Preheat the oven to 425°F then mix the flour, cornmeal, sugar and baking powder together in a bowl. Mix the eggs, milk and oil together in a separate bowl then pour over the dry ingredients. Stir the batter just enough to mix it well.

Pour into a greased, 9" square baking pan and bake for 25 to 30 minutes or until the top is lightly browned. Serve while still warm.

This recipe is presented by Bonnie Burke who runs heritage cooking classes at this delightful museum. Called the Harvest Home Program, it was developed for children. Through discussion and participation, children learn to compare our Thanksgiving Harvest traditions to those of the mid-19th century. Emphasis is on the contributions made by native people. Visitors should make a point of visiting the museum to learn more about Brockville and the history of the 1,000 Islands.

The railway tunnel

Canada's oldest underground railway tunnel was built between 1854 and 1860 in Brockville. This 1,730 foot long tunnel runs from Brockville's waterfront north for four blocks.

Despite financial problems, the tunnel was completed and used for 100 years. The last train rumbled through the tunnel in 1969; by 1976 the tracks were removed.

During the summer months, the bright red caboose, preserved at the tunnel site, is a favorite among visitors. It has information panels about the tunnel. The interior of the caboose has been fully restored as a working railway car.

Oven Fried Potatoes

Presented by Nancy Webster, Lansdowne

Ingredients:

8 large potatoes	1/2 cup of oil
2 tbsp of grated Parmesan cheese	1 tsp of salt
1/2 tsp of garlic powder	1/2 tsp of paprika
1/4 tsp of pepper	

Method:

Preheat the oven to 375°F. Cut each potato into 8 wedges and, in 2 shallow baking pans, arrange so the peel side is down. Mix the remaining ingredients and brush over the potatoes. Bake for 45 minutes or until the potatoes are golden brown and tender. Brush occasionally with the oil mixture.

Eric and Nancy Webster neé Purvis live on one of the family's farms at Greenfield in the Lansdowne area. Their century farm is now operated by their son, George, and his wife, Rebecca. Both Nancy and Eric are descended from old Leeds County families.

A strange harvest

Two brothers nicknamed Wick and Allie were undaunted by marsh hay which carpeted much of their poorly drained farm, north of the village of Lansdowne. Now marsh hay, or 'redtop', has little animal food value. However, it does have a fine, soft stem which makes it excellent packing material.

Wick and Allie discovered that large mail order enterprises, such as Eatons and Simpsons, needed packing material to cushion glass during shipment.

Ralph Smith of Lansdowne remembers that Wick and Allie shipped several freight car loads of redtop bales to Toronto each year. And he recalls dishes from Simpsons, packed in Wick and Allie's redtop, arriving in his mother's kitchen.

The brothers harvested and shipped their redtop to Toronto until the early 1930's when they died, hours apart. Their passing was marked by a double funeral.

61

Purchase by barter

Thomas Darling, in the early part of the 19th century, established and operated a store and wood station to supply fuel to steamers on the St. Lawrence River. The building still stands, just east of the 1,000 Islands International Bridge.

Barter seems to have been a significant part of the Darling family's enterprise. Here is a partial list of commodities or services used to discharge debts.

Cordwood, a load of hay, plastering the store, 6 bushels of wheat for feeding oxen, 200 feet of lumber, a few fine fish, silver watch, 3 bushels of ashes, 13 days laber (sic), 1 bushel of peas, 2 stacks of hay, and by going to Gananque.

The customer who discharged his account by "going to Gananoque" – a distance of some 12 miles each way, obviously anticipated the modern courier companies.

Tomato-Fruit Sauce
Presented by Blu Mackintosh, Ivy Lea

Ingredients:

10 ripe tomatoes, chopped
2 medium onions
2 cups of white sugar
1/2 tsp of salt
1 tsp each of nutmeg, cinnamon and allspice

4 pears, peaches or apples
2 cups of brown sugar
2 cups of cider vinegar

Method:

Peel the pears/peaches/apples, remove seeds and pits and dice. Both onions should be peeled and chopped.

Combine the ingredients in a large, stainless steel or enamel pot and cook slowly for 1 hour or until thick. Stir from time to time to prevent sticking, especially toward the end of the cooking time. Pour into sterilized jars and seal.

This sauce goes well with cold meat and is a great way to use up a glut of tomatoes. Mixed into some softened cream cheese, it makes a good spread or dip. Add some ginger or curry if you want it to be more like a chutney.

Blu Mackintosh is the chair person of fund raising for the Thousand Islands Foundation for the Performing Arts (the Thousand Islands Playhouse) in Gananoque. She was board president from 1988 to 1992.

Spiced Grape Punch

Presented by Manse Lane Bed & Breakfast
465 Stone Street South, Gananoque

Ingredients:

1 1/2 cups of sugar	2 or 3 cinnamon sticks
2 tsp of whole cloves	3 cups of water
6 cups of apple juice	
12 oz of frozen grape juice concentrate, thawed	

Method:

Combine the sugar, cinnamon sticks, whole cloves and 3 cups of water in a saucepan. Heat, stirring constantly until boiling. Simmer 5 minutes. Let stand 15 minutes then strain into a small bowl. Discard the spices.

Just before serving, stir the syrup into 3 cups of hot water. Stir in the grape juice and apple juice. Garnish with lemon slices and serve warm. The syrup may be kept in the refrigerator for at least 1 month.

The Manse Lane Bed and Breakfast is owned by Jocelyn and George Bounds. Guests are served a full breakfast between 8 and 9:30 a.m. Picnic lunches are available upon request. Manse Lane offers a smoke-free environment.

Gananoque's founder

Joel Stone was born in Gilford, Connecticut in 1749. American authorities imprisoned him for his loyalty to England's King and, as a United Empire Loyalist, he fled to Canada where he was granted large tracts of land on the Gananoque River.

Stone and his family relied upon the river to power various industrial enterprises including a lumber mill which began operations in 1759.

Stone generally is accorded the title of Gananoque's Founder. He operated a number of commercial enterprises and represented the colonial government in various capacities.

He died in 1833 at 84 years of age.

Getting his feet wet

Young Joel Parmenter left home in Stockbridge, Vermont in 1824. Canada bound, he arrived at Clayton, NY and engaged a pair of local river men to ferry him to Gananoque by canoe.

Poor Joel was unused to the craft. He stepped in one side and was pitched out the other, into the river. Alarmed, the canoeists revised the contractual arrangement and required Joel to lie quietly on the canoe's floor.

At Gananoque, he became a successful merchant and hotel keeper. His limestone house, now The Golden Apple Restaurant, has long been a well known attraction.

The house stayed in Joel's family for years. In 1928, Katherine Runyan of New Jersey opened The Golden Apple Restaurant, named for an apple orchard probably planted by Gananoque's founder, Col. Joel Stone. The orchard is gone but the restaurant has been a landmark for almost seven decades.

Plum Gumbo

Presented by The Golden Apple Restaurant
45 King Street West, Gananoque

Editors' Note:

This old recipe is for a sauce for meats. It was made at The Golden Apple Restaurant for years and was very popular.

Ingredients:

5 lb of prune plums	2 lb of seeded raisins
3 oranges	1 lemon
5 lb of sugar	1/2 lb of chopped walnuts

Method:

Wash the plums, remove the stones then cut the plums into pieces. Wipe the oranges and lemon, cut into thin slices then chop finely and remove the seeds. Place the fruit in a kettle and add the sugar. Bring to the boiling point and let simmer, stirring often, until the mixture has the consistency of marmalade. Add the chopped nuts last. Bottle and seal.

The Golden Apple Restaurant today is owned by Shirley and Sil Fernetich. For almost 70 years, The Golden Apple has been the place to break your journey between Montreal and Toronto. There are three, separate dining rooms and a tree-shaded patio. The dining rooms are decorated with many Victorian items.

Poached Eggs with Maple Syrup

Presented by Marion Steacy, Gananoque

Ingredients:

1 1/2 cups of maple syrup   eggs
bacon   baked beans

Method:

Heat the maple syrup to the boiling point. Add the eggs and poach them until they are cooked. Remove the eggs with a spatula and serve them with bacon and baked beans. Pour a little maple syrup over everything and enjoy.

Marion Steacy is a retired school teacher and business person. She lived in Warburton, north of Lansdowne, after her marriage, but today lives in Gananoque.

The price of education

Young Marion Steacy wanted to teach but the cost of an education was beyond her means. So she turned to her father, Bland Webster, who sold a prize cow to finance her wardrobe and higher education. This enabled Marion to follow a family tradition; her mother, Julia Washburn, also was a teacher.

Marion earned the magnificent sum of $475 for her first year of teaching at the one-room Greenfield School. Her students included her brothers and cousins. Her recollection of her first day as a new teacher is still vivid. A cousin sustained a facial cut, confronting Marion with a medical crisis before the opening bell.

Her teaching career spanned 30 years. And for 27 years, she owned and operated a school bus line. Her first bus was a converted bread truck. Marion learned to drive at age 12.

Dining at Shipman's

Shipman's Dining Room at The Glen House Resort is named after the original settlers of this property. The Shipman family were United Empire Loyalists who turned the land into a prosperous farm.

About 1875, the first vacationing fisherman arrived at The Glen House from the railhead at Clayton, New York about nine miles by steam launch.

By the early 1900's, the 1,000 Islands had earned a reputation as a playground for the wealthy. Among the famous names were Seagram, Wiser, Vanderbilt, Rubenstein, Benson and Pullman. Some fine old family mansions still stand and can be seen by taking one of the many boat tours which ply the island waters.

66

Chicken Oscar
Presented by The Glen House Resort, 1,000 Islands Parkway

Ingredients:

4 boneless chicken breasts
2 cups of crab meat or imitation crab meat
2 cups of mushrooms
2 cups of Béarnaise sauce*
16 fresh asparagus spears (or one can)

Editors' Note:

To create Béarnaise sauce, begin with Hollandaise (see recipe on page 21). Simmer 2 tbsp of chopped shallots, scallions or small white onions and 1/2 tsp of dried tarragon in 2 tbsp of dry white wine until the wine evaporates in 2 or 3 minutes. Add this mixture, and freshly ground black pepper, to warm, stiff Hollandaise and you have Béarnaise sauce.

Method:

Pan fry the chicken breasts. Layer crabmeat and the mushrooms and asparagus spears on top of the cooked chicken breasts. Coat with hot Bearnaise sauce and place under the broiler for 1 minute.

The Glen House Resort has been operated by the Seal family since 1963. Located on the bank of the St. Lawrence River, The Glen House is located in the heart of the 1,000 Islands. This recipe was supplied by chef Jackie McNeil. The Glen House is owned by the same Seal family which owns and operates the Blinkbonnie in Gananoque.

Sausage and Sauce

Presented by Barbara McAllister, Gananoque

Ingredients:

1 lb link sausage	1 large onion
1 large tin of tomatoes	1 tin of cut mushrooms
3 stalks of celery, chopped	1/2 green pepper, chopped
1 clove of garlic	salt and pepper to taste

Method:

Simmer the sausages in water for 10 minutes. Pour off the fat and water. Brown the sausages in a pan then add onions, celery and garlic. Cook until tender then add green pepper, mushrooms and tomatoes. Add seasoning, cover and simmer for 30 minutes. Serves 6.

Barbara was born in Kingston and grew up on the family farm in nearby Joyceville. She is a natural story teller and freelance writer.

A WEST SIDE STORY!

Gananoque's founder, Colonel Joel Stone, once offered a bounty for crows' heads – 25 cents if the crow was shot on the east side of the Gananoque River but only 20 cents if shot on the west side.

Thaddeus Leavitt, author of the History of Leeds and Grenville 1749–1879, *was blessed with a wry sense of humor which caused him to write: "It is unnecessary to state that not a single crow met its death on the west side."*

A prisoner for love

Eunice Whiting was, by all accounts, a lovely young woman. She stood 5 feet 1 inch in height, had a fair complexion, dark eyes and auburn hair. Sadly, she was a horse thief sentenced in June of 1839 to three years in Kingston Penitentiary.

And Eunice was the lover of one of the leaders of what had come to be called The Patriot's Rebellion of 1837–1838. Self-styled patriots sought to 'free' the Canadian colony from British bonds.

"… the young amazon (Eunice–ed.) was employed as a courier in the patriot cause to carry communication from one party to another – sometimes dressed as a boy and sometimes as a girl, she has been known to ride 50 and 60 miles a day," wrote Captain David Ballingall of the British Royal Marines. He visited Kingston Penitentiary in 1842.

Continued on the next page

Mushroom Caviar
Presented by Casablanca Gourmet Bed & Breakfast
Highway 2, near Kingston

Ingredients:

3 medium onions, minced	5 tbsp of virgin olive oil
1 1/2 lb of fresh mushrooms	4 tsp of ground coriander seeds
salt	fresh black pepper
chopped parsley	thinly sliced black bread

Method:

Cook the onions in hot oil until they are soft. Meanwhile, wash and chop the mushrooms finely. Add the coriander, salt and pepper to taste and cook until the mushrooms release their juice. Turn up the heat so most of the liquid evaporates.

Refrigerate to chill. Check the seasoning. To serve, decorate with parsley and serve with black bread.

Serves 12 as an hors d'oeuvre.

The Casablanca Gourmet Bed & Breakfast is more than a wonderful place to unwind and relax. It offers gourmet dinner and a wide range of cooking classes (hands-on or demonstrations) by Marcel Bahri, a European-trained professional chef. Marcel and Ruth, your hosts, are bilingual in French and English and speak some German and Spanish as well.

Corn Crusted Chicken

Presented by Chez Piggy Restaurant, 68-R Princess Street, Kingston

Editors' Note:

Please see the "Grazing" section for the Black Bean Salad recipe which should be served with this dish.

Ingredients:

fresh greens or lettuce   4 chicken breasts, skin on

1/2 lb of grated, smoked gruyère cheese

Ingredients for the Marinade:

2 sliced garlic cloves	1 tsp of chili powder
1/2 tsp of paprika	1 tsp of ground cumin
1/2 tsp of ground pepper	1/4 tsp of salt
3 tbsp of olive oil	

Ingredients for the Corn Crust:

1/2 cup of corn meal	1 tbsp of chopped parsley
1 tsp of dried thyme	

Method:

Mix the spices with the olive oil and rub on the chicken breasts as a marinade. Dip the marinated chicken breasts in the corn meal mixture, fry, turning once, until cooked, about 20 minutes. To serve, place the Black Bean Salad on a plate and top with sliced corn crusted chicken breasts, then the smoked cheese. Add a few greens as a garnish. Serves 4.

Chez Piggy offers imaginative, international cuisine complemented by an extensive wine list. A cozy limestone interior and landscaped garden make it an attractive place for formal dining or casual snacks. All desserts and breads are baked daily at its bakery, Pan Chancho, 70 Johnson Street. Many of Chez Piggy's desserts and other menu items are available there for take-out as well as a wide selection of salads, patés and imported cheeses. The chef is Victoria Newbury; co-owners are Rose Richardson and Zal Yanovsky.

Continued from the previous page

The good Captain was obviously taken with Eunice for he wrote: "… she is only 18 years of age – consequently little more than 15 when she was tried – poor girl she is much to be pitied, her crime arose, not from any attachment to the political principals of her lover – but from a pure and youthful affection to the object of all others she held most dear on earth."

But Eunice, and another convict named Roda Morrison, became the first prisoners to escape from the limestone fortress on the night of Dec. 17–18, 1839. The Kingston Chronicle & Gazette *reported that Eunice "is said to be of prepossessing appearance". Nothing is reported about Roda Morrison other than her age (16) and that she was "belonging to Kingston".*

Both were recaptured on Dec. 19th by Warden H. Smith, his two sons and a prison guard. The escapees were discovered, concealed, in Kingston Township.

Warden Smith asked his superiors for permission to pay a promised reward to the informant who 'ratted out' Eunice and Roda, "as I expect an application for the payment of the same tomorrow."

Truly, there is no honor among thieves.

Seven generations

Seven generations of the Clark family have lived in this house built in 1832 by Anthony McGuin. The family has been linked to several thriving businesses including three mills during the 19th century. During the 1920's and '30's, the house was known as Loyalist Lodge.

Early in this century, Harold Clark, grandfather of the present owners, operated an ice cream factory and it is believed that maple walnut ice cream was invented here.

It was near here that Geoffrey O'Hara wrote the World War I era song K-K-K-Katy, 'as the m-m-m-moon shines over the (Clark family's) cowshed ...'. O'Hara invited Katy Craig to a party; he began to compose the popular song as he waited for her to dress.

The main building is constructed from limestone. Today, period furnishings reflect the elegance expected of one of Canada's top 100 restaurants.

Stuffed Venison Tenderloin with a Cranberry Five Peppercorn Sauce

Presented by Clark's by the Bay, 4085 Bath Road, Kingston

Ingredients:

two 1 1/2 lb venison tenderloins

Ingredients for the Stuffing:

3 cups of cubed, whole wheat bread   1 1/2 cups of diced Ida Red apples
2 garlic cloves, finely chopped   1/4 cup of olive oil
1 tsp each of fresh oregano, thyme, rosemary and summer savory
1 1/2 tsp of fresh ground peppercorns (green, pink, black, white, Jamaican)

Ingredients for Cranberry Peppercorn Sauce:

1 1/2 oz of Calvados   4 oz of dried cranberries*
2 1/2 cups of whipping cream   1 1/2 tsp of fresh peppercorn mix
salt to taste
1 cup of good Canadian dry red wine†
1/2 tsp each of fresh oregano, rosemary, thyme and summer savory

*or 8 oz of fresh cranberries
†either Cave Spring or Lakeview Cellars

Continued on the next page

Continued from the previous page

Method:
Preheat the oven to 350°F. Slice the tenderloins to facilitate pounding then flatten each to approximately 1/8" thickness.

To create the stuffing, mix the ingredients and place the mixture on the flattened meat. Roll each tenderloin around the stuffing using a skewer to hold it together. Brown the tenderloins quickly in a large frying pan. Remove and place them in a roasting pan when browned. Pour 3 oz of Calvados over top and place the roasting pan in the oven for 45 minutes to 1 hour.

While the tenderloins are in the oven, deglaze the frying pan with Calvados. Add the red wine, herbs, peppercorns and cranberries and reduce this mixture by half. Add the whipping cream and reduce again until it coats the back of your spoon.

Remove the meat from the oven when ready and cut 3/4" slices from the rolled tenderloins. Spoon the sauce onto the plate, then top with the sliced tenderloins.

If venison tenderloins are not available, pork or veal can be substituted.

Clark's by the Bay is owned by Clark, Laurie and David Day. The chef is Jofus (Jack) Francis. Clark's by the Bay is listed in 100 Best Restaurants of Canada *and* Where to Eat in Canada. *It is a four diamond award winner. The historic building overlooks scenic Collins Bay. Small rooms, open fireplaces and period furnishing combined with wonderful cuisine and fine service make this one of the country's top restaurants.*

Early cosmetics

Excerpts from The Home Cook Book *by the Ladies of Toronto and Chief Cities and Towns in Canada, 1877.*

COLD CREAM
Four ounces sweet almond oil, two ounces of rose water, two ounces of white wax, two ounces of cocoa butter, two of spermaceti; put in a bowl in a pan of boiling water; cut the spermaceti, white wax, and cocoa butter in small pieces; put them in the bowl, also the oil and rose water. When melted, stir contents until cold.

EXCELLENT FAMILY SOAP
One box of lye, five pounds of grease, one pound of resin, one and a half gallons of soft water; make in an iron pot. When the water boils, put in the lye, when this is dissolved add the grease; stir till all is melted; then add one pound of resin gradually, and boil for an hour and a half; keep stirring with a stick, and add hot water to keep up the original quantity; pour into wet tins, and let it stand for twenty-four hours; cut into bars and keep in a dry warm place for a month.

Welcome back ospreys

Ospreys, large 'fish hawks', are returning to the 1,000 Islands ecosystem. Their numbers had dwindled, but thanks to the cooperative effort of the Canadian Parks Service, Canadian Wildlife Service and the Ontario Ministry of Natural Resources, they have been lured back with 'free housing'.

This trio of agencies established a number of nesting platforms where ospreys lay their two to four eggs in a mass of sticks and debris mounted atop telephone poles, high above the water.

The poles have been mounted on small islets and rocky shoals. These nesting platforms replace the tall, mature dead trees – the ospreys' nesting location of preference – which no longer are as common as they once were.

The ospreys' diet is fish and nothing but.

MicMac Spareribs
Presented by Larry McMillan, Gananoque

Ingredients:

1 onion	2 tsp of salt
1/4 tsp of pepper	
4 lb of spareribs cracked in half, length-wise	

Ingredients for the Sauce:

1/2 cup of cider vinegar	1/2 cup of brown sugar (packed)
1/2 cup of ketchup	1/2 cup of chili sauce
1/4 cup of Worcestershire sauce	2 tbsp of chopped onions
1 tbsp of lemon juice	1/2 tsp of dry mustard
1 crushed garlic clove	cayenne pepper to taste

Method:

In a large kettle, place the ribs, onions (quartered), salt and pepper. Cover with water, bring to a boil and reduce the heat. Simmer covered for 1 1/2 hours or until very tender. Drain but make sure you do not lose the onions.

The sauce may be made while the ribs are cooking. In a medium saucepan, combine all the sauce ingredients and simmer for at least 1 hour, or until the sauce thickens to a consistency slightly thicker than ketchup.

Continued on the next page

Continued from the previous page

Arrange the ribs on a tray and cover thoroughly with the sauce. Barbecue until the ribs are heated through. Baste often with extra sauce. In winter, use your broiler but turn the ribs frequently and remember to baste them with extra sauce. Because of the sugar content of the sauce, it may burn easily in the broiler so rotate and baste often.

A Postscript:
Sometimes Larry quadruples the sauce ingredients. He funnels the excess into an old, squeezable plastic bottle for use as barbecue sauce. If you follow suit, remember to cut the onions small enough to pass through the spout of a squeeze bottle. The sauce assumes a new flavor when cooked a second time.

By day, Larry is a graphic designer; at night he transforms into MicMac (his Internet name), the computer consultant. The name of this dish is his shameless and blatant advertisement for his moonlight activities. We include it only because of its redeeming culinary value and because he is a very user-friendly person who interfaces well with his friends.

This is an old family recipe which Larry reveals here for the first time.

Larry and his Macintosh computer share life with his patient and understanding wife, Mary, two sons, Joshua and Adam, and a cat named Yoda.

The mighty river

The St. Lawrence is the 17th largest river in the world in terms of volume. It is the principal outlet of the Great Lakes, the world's largest supply of fresh water, and it links the continent's heartland to the Atlantic Ocean.

In the 18th century, the river was a highway for bateaux, flat bottomed boats of 30 or 40 feet in length. These vessels were pointed at each end and carried more than four tons of freight. They were powered by sail, oars or towing, depending upon weather, wind and current conditions.

Typically, the trip from Montreal to Kingston, against the current, was ten to twelve days. The return trip, however, required only three or four days.

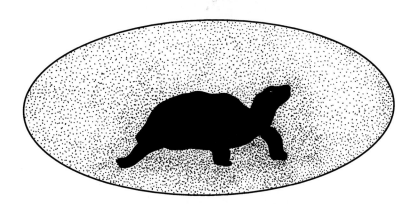

Symbols of the river

Visitors and residents of the 1,000 Islands inevitably think of the great blue heron as the symbol of this marvellous region. This stately fisherman can reach 52 inches in height and has a wingspan which can stretch to 70 inches.

Great blues fly with their necks folded, but for all their grace and beauty, their voice is a guttural squawk as anyone who has ever startled one can attest .

With characteristic patience, great blues wade the shallows. A lightning-like lunge usually is deadly for a fish or frog, the meals of preference. Herons often stand, sentinel-like, on the end of docks, atop rocky shoals or in the branches of trees which may overhang the water.

They nest in colonies and lay their three to five eggs on a platform of sticks lined with soft material.

Ham Muffins
Presented by Mayone Kelly, Marble Rock Road

Ingredients:

1/4 cup of butter	1 well beaten egg
1 cup of graham flour	1 cup of white flour
3 tsp of baking powder	1 cup of milk
3/4 cup of cooked ham, finely chopped	

Method:

Cream the butter, add the ham, egg, then alternately the graham flour and white flour which has been sifted with the baking powder. Add the milk, mix well and bake in a well buttered muffin pan for 25 minutes at 350°F.

Mayone Kelly offers this recipe from an old, cloth-covered cook book which she has owned for years. Frankly, we couldn't decide how to classify this dish so we placed it in the "Great Expectations" section on the assumption that these ham muffins might go well as an accompaniment to a main meal in place of bread.

Angel Hair Pasta with Shrimp

Presented by The Blinkbonnie Motor Lodge, 50 Main Street, Gananoque

Ingredients:

1 1/2 tbsp of butter	1 1/2 tbsp of flour
1 1/2 cups of milk	1/2 cup of 35% cream
1 1/2 tbsp of pesto sauce	1 1/2 tbsp of chopped parsley
1 tbsp of minced garlic	2 tbsp of grated parmesan cheese
1/2 tsp of salt	1/2 tsp of white pepper
Worcestershire and Tabasco	1/2 red pepper cut in strips
1/4 lb of trimmed snow peas	1 lb of jumbo shrimp
0.67 lb of capellini or enough to serve 4	

Method:

In a saucepan over medium heat, melt butter, stir in flour and cook for a few minutes until golden. Add milk and cream, bring to a gentle simmer and continue to stir until thickened. Add pesto, parsley, garlic, parmesan, salt, pepper, Worcestershire and Tabasco, and stir until blended. Reduce heat and keep warm, stirring occasionally.

Cook the pasta quickly in a large pot of boiling water for 3 to 4 minutes, or until *al dente*. At the same time, poach the pepper, snow peas and shrimp in another pot of boiling water (2 or 3 minutes, or until just heated through). Drain the pasta, mix it with the sauce and portion it into heated individual serving bowls. Garnish each portion with shrimp and vegetables and serve immediately.

Serves 4.

The Blinkbonnie Motor Lodge has long been associated with tourism in Gananoque. The Seal family purchased it in 1983. Renovations turned this 19th century home into an excellent establishment which offers some of the finest dining in town. This recipe was submitted by chef Jackie McNeil.

Historic dining

In 1810, merchant Charles McDonald came from New York State to Gananoque where he prospered. He built a frame home in 1812 which burned in 1828. It was replaced in 1843.

Today, The Blinkbonnie *incorporates that 1843 structure including many alterations and expansions.*

Members of Mr. McDonald's family lived at The Blinkbonnie *until the 1920's when it was purchased by Rebecca Edwards, a Kingston school teacher. She was the first to operate* The Blinkbonnie *as a tourist home.*

Miss Edwards operated the establishment until 1955. During the '50's, a 32-unit motel was added but the business changed hands several times during the 60's and 70's. It was acquired and restored in 1983 by the Seal family.

75

Sighing swains?

Excerpts from the History of Leeds and Grenville 1749–1879 *by Thaddeus Leavitt.*

"Among the pioneers, great difficulty was for many years experienced in the consummation of courtship, the Rev. Dr. Stuart being the only regular clergyman from the Lower Province line to Kingston. Sighing swains were compelled to wait for months, and in some cases for years, before the golden opportunity presented itself ... The ladies of ye olden time, and particularly the brides, were dressed in a style essentially different from those shown in the fashion plates of the Bazar for 1878. Fancy bonnets, kid gloves, and silk dresses were never dreamed of. The most complete wardrobe consisted of a home-spun dress, deer-skin petticoats, dyed blue from the bark of the soft maple, and a squirrel-skin bonnet. In many instances, bride and bridegroom mounted the same horse, and rode away to the nearest magistrate, a happy couple."

Sauce for Fettuccine Alfredo
Presented by Aunt Lucy's, 1399 Princess Street, Kingston

Ingredients:

1/4 lb of real butter	1/4 cup of whipping cream
1/2 cup of grated Parmesan cheese	1/2 tsp of chopped garlic
1/2 tsp of thyme	

Method:

Melt the butter, add the cream slowly and stir constantly. Add the garlic and thyme and bring the mixture to a boil. Add the cheese slowly and keep stirring until the boil resumes then reduce the heat to very low and make sure that all the cheese is melted, about 5 minutes.

Ingredients for the Microwave Version:

1/2 cup of butter	1/2 cup of whipping cream
1 cup of grated Parmesan cheese	

Method:

Cut the butter into small pieces in a bowl suitable for use in a microwave oven then add the cheese and cream. Cook on 'high' for about 1 minute; stir and repeat.

Editors' Note:

For a delicious, rich pasta dish, mix this sauce with fettuccine.

Aunt Lucy's has been a Kingston tradition and landmark since 1947. While dining is casual, the food and service are first-rate. Private booths with tapestry upholstered benches, lace curtains, tiffany lamps and stencilled chairs in rose and teal impart a country inn ambiance to the dining room. All dishes are prepared with only the finest and freshest ingredients. Aunt Lucy's is open 7 days a week and is owned by Gerry Warne.

Great Grazing

salad, soup & chowder

Mo's Beer Bottle Salad Baster

Presented by Mo Bock, Marble Rock Road

Editors' Note:
This is a salad dressing. We thought we should tell you that up front ... just in case you wondered.

Ingredients:

1 bottle of Grolsch beer	olive oil
balsamic vinegar	ketchup
mustard	barbecue sauce
juice from olive jars, pickle jars etc.	

Method:
The key to this special sauce is the container — an empty Grolsch bottle (resealable and infinitely reusable, hence environmentally friendly to boot). First, drink the Grolsch. Do not rinse the bottle. Fill it roughly one-third full of olive oil. Add another third of balsamic or your flavor of choice.

Now add vinegar and the ingredients: mustard from a squeeze bottle ("count wunsey, toosey"); ketchup from a squeeze bottle ("again ... wunsey, toosey"); barbecue sauce ("same drill") then dribble in juice from olive jars, pickle jars, etc. Now shake the bottle. You will find that you have to shake it every time you pour.

Finally, drink the other Grolsch, they come in packs of two. Do rinse the second bottle, unless you plan to mix a batch for a friend. Fiddle with the proportions until you find exactly the right blend for your taste.

The full name for this elixir is "Mo Bock's 'Mo' Better Beer Bottle Salad Baster" (sorry Mo, we ran out of space!). Mo is a talented actor and fixture at the Thousand Islands Playhouse in Gananoque and has been since its inception in 1982. His swashbuckling villain, Rupert, in The Prisoner of Zenda *is our favorite Mo role. Acting, directing, renovating and occasionally administering keep him almost too busy to eat. But when he does, he likes to prepare this tangy salad dressing which goes with almost any salad you can think of ... and then some.*

Flower power

This recipe for dandelion cordial comes from the Purity Flour Cookbook *of 1923, published by Western Canada Flour Mills Co. Ltd. The book is owned by Mayone Kelly of Marble Rock whose recipes and exploits appear elsewhere in this book.*

Ingredients:
2 qt of dandelion blossoms
4 qt of boiling water
3 lb of sugar
2 oranges
1 lemon

Pour the boiling water over the dandelion blossoms and let stand overnight. Strain then add the sugar dissolved in boiling water. Add the thinly sliced oranges and lemon and let stand for three days. Strain before serving.

79

Maple Sugaring, 1841

Excerpts from the diary of British Royal Marines Captain David Ballingall, 1841.

"Since I have been in this country I have always expressed great desire to witness the process of obtaining the sap from the Maple Tree from which Sugar is manufactured. Major Logie, an officer who had seen a great deal of service and who sold his commission came to this country ten years since as a settler – His place is called Glenlogie, beautifully situated on the St. Lawrence about five miles from Kingston. As he has on his settlement what is termed a Sugar Bush, he kindly offered to gratify my curiosity.

"Accordingly we set out ... in a large farming sleigh ... I was much pleased with the patient docility of his two fine oxen that drew the sleigh; The caution evinced by the animals when they came to a part where they considered the

Continued on the next page

1,000 Islands Salad Dressing

Presented by: Trinity House Inn, 90 Stone Street South, Gananoque

Editors' Note:

On page 2, we shared the results of our research into the origin of 1,000 Islands Salad Dressing. Just to muddy the waters, here is another version.

Ingredients:

1 pint of Mayonnaise	4 oz of chili sauce
1 tbsp of chopped parsley	2 tbsp of chopped onions
1 tbsp of chopped green pepper	1 tbsp of chopped dill pickle
1 tbsp of chopped gherkin pickles	2 chopped hard-boiled eggs
dash of lemon juice	salt and pepper to taste
1 tbsp of chopped green olives (stuffed)	

Method:

Combine ingredients in a blender. Keep refrigerated.

Trinity House Inn is a luxurious, award winning inn. A dignified Victorian, the house announces its presence with symmetry and balance. The eight-room inn has been restored with modern amenities added and it is sure to appeal to the sophisticated traveller. Guests can relax on a private deck overlooking a waterfall garden. For those who appreciate old-world charm and hospitality in elegant surroundings, Trinity House Inn is the answer.

Marinated Endive Salad

Presented by Trinity House Inn, 90 Stone Street South, Gananoque

Ingredients:

1 cup of olive oil   1/3 cup of red wine vinegar

1 tbsp of balsamic vinegar   endive lettuce

1/4 cup crushed, blanched almonds   salt and pepper to taste

3 garlic cloves, crushed and finely chopped

sliced black olives and Italian plum tomatoes

Method:

Combine the oil, vinegars, garlic, almonds and spices in a blender. Wash the endive lettuce then toss with the dressing. Allow it to marinate in the refrigerator for at least 1/2 hour, but no longer than 2 hours. On service, garnish with black olives and tomatoes.

This salad is an ideal companion for a pasta dish.

Trinity House Inn has an imaginative menu featuring modern country house cuisine. The dining bistro offers two dining rooms and a verandah. There is a lounge for guests of the inn.

Continued from previous page

snow to be too deep for them they would stand and look at their driver, who they seemed to regard as a friend, and carefully listen to his voice, as to which way they were to proceed ... A hole is bored with an auger about an inch deep ... But I understand in most parts of the United States, the method is much handier, a nail is driven into the hole just below the spout and on this the Bucket is hung by a hole in one of the staves – The advantages are that a shorter spout serves, and the sap cannot be overturned by the hogs or stray cattle, as it frequently is when it stands upon the ground ... About two to three hundred trees generally compose a Sugar Bush ... but sometimes a thousand are tapped ... The men carry a couple of pails suspended from each end of a yoke fitted on their shoulders as our milkmen carry their pails at home ... the Sap is a pleasant drink, perceptibly sweet, very cool and refreshing and not the least cloying ... A tree will produce from two to four pounds of Sugar in a favorable season ... It is sold at Kingston at 5 shillings per pound ... the country people have it to give a relish to the bread with their tea, and it is considered very healthy to the children who are excessively fond of it in this form."

People of the islands

The French discovered the region and named it Les Milles Isles *— the 1,000 Islands. The period of French influence lasted to 1763. Next came the United Empire Loyalists from 1783 until the early part of the 19th century.*

The American Revolution triggered the exodus of some 50,000 loyalists from England's former 13 colonies. Many left the fledgling American republic they were persecuted for their British sympathies. Most of the earliest settlers were soldiers and their families.

Their loyalty was rewarded with free land, as much as 1,000 acres for a field officer, 700 for a captain, 500 for subalterns, staff and warrant officers while non-commissioned officers received 200. Private soldiers received 100 acres each. Each member of a soldier's family received 100 acres. Heads of non-combatant families received 100 acres, others got 50 acres. These amounts were increased in 1788 to encourage settlement.

Broccoli Salad
Presented by Louise Baldree, Gananoque

Ingredients:

1 bunch of broccoli*
1/2 cup of sultana raisins
1 cup of Miracle Whip
2 tbsp of lemon juice

1/2 cup of chopped pecans
8 crisp bacon slices, crumbled
1/2 cup of white sugar

*The broccoli should be chopped finely; a food processor is perfect for this.

Editors' Note:

At social events, Louise's broccoli salad is one of the first dishes to disappear! It has become a favorite of ours and best of all ... it doesn't even look or taste like broccoli. Even George Bush would approve.

Method:

Mix the Miracle Whip, sugar and lemon juice. This is better if it is made a day ahead.

Pour the dressing over the broccoli, pecans, raisins and crumbled bacon and stir in. Refrigerate. Serves 6.

Louise Baldree owns Baldree's Your Independent Grocer in partnership with her husband, Bev, and son, Scott. She has three children and six grandchildren. Louise enjoys reading and her family says she is a wonderful cook.

Caesar Salad for Two

Presented by The General Wolfe Hotel, Wolfe Island

Ingredients:

salt and freshly ground pepper
1 anchovy filet
1 tbsp of white vinegar
1 tbsp of red wine vinegar
2 tbsp of olive oil
garlic cloves
1 head of romaine lettuce, rinsed and dried

1 egg yolk
1/2 lemon
1 tbsp of dijon mustard
1 tbsp of grated parmesan cheese
2 tbsp of croutons

Method:

Season a large, wooden bowl with white salt and freshly ground pepper. Mash garlic cloves and the anchovy filet into a smooth paste.

Add both vinegars, olive oil, the egg yolk and mustard. Squeeze in the lemon juice and whip the mixture vigorously to a light, creamy sauce. Toss in bite-sized cuts of romaine until they glisten. Sprinkle the parmesan cheese and croutons on top; toss gently and serve.

Miro and Hana Zborovsky are your hosts at this 135 year old hotel which is famous for its award-winning gourmet dinners and spectacular view of Kingston's skyline. The 20-minute ferry ride to Wolfe Island will whet your appetite for a spectacular meal.

A major trade route

The St. Lawrence River was named by French explorer Jacques Cartier in 1535. He arrived in the Gulf of St. Lawrence on August 10, the date on the ecclesiastical calendar which commemorated the martyrdom of Saint Lawrence.

Since its discovery, nearly 500 years ago, The St. Lawrence River has served as a highway for trade. By 1800, early settlers of the region were shipping agricultural surpluses to Montreal in freight-carrying bateaux. There, bateaux were loaded with imported goods for a return trip upriver.

Bateaux were replaced by Durham boats which held larger cargoes and reflected increased trade volume. The first Durham boat left Kingston in 1801. Durham boats were replaced by steamers as the century progressed. In 1959, the St. Lawrence Seaway was completed allowing seagoing vessels access to ports along the Great Lakes.

Black Bean Salad

Presented by Chez Piggy Restaurant, 68-R Princess Street, Kingston

Ingredients:

1/2 lb of dried black beans
1 tsp of whole cumin
1 bay leaf
1/4 cup of diced green pepper
2 fresh minced chilies
4 diced tomatoes
4 more garlic cloves, chopped
2 tbsp each of lemon, lime and orange zest

1 tbsp of salt
2 garlic cloves, chopped
1/4 cup of diced red onion
1/4 cup of chopped fresh coriander
1/2 cup of lime juice
1/4 cup of olive oil

Method:

Slowly simmer the beans, cumin, 2 garlic cloves and bay leaf in water with 1 tbsp of salt until soft. Take care not to over-cook the beans. Drain and rinse them in cold water and remove the bay leaf. Add the cooled beans to the remaining ingredients, season to taste and chill.

Serve with the corn crusted chicken recipe on page 69 in the Great Expectations section.

Once it was a livery stable, today, Chez Piggy offers imaginative, international cuisine complemented by an extensive wine list. A cozy limestone interior and landscaped garden make it an attractive place for formal dining or casual snacks. All desserts and breads are baked daily at its bakery, Pan Chancho, 70 Johnson Street. Many of Chez Piggy's desserts and other menu items are available there for take-out as well as a wide selection of salads, patés and imported cheeses. The chef is Victoria Newbury; co-owners are Rose Richardson and Zal Yanovsky.

A growing economy

The United Empire Loyalists cleared their lands and planted their crops. Toward the end of the 18th century they actually had surplus goods which were shipped to Montreal, down the St. Lawrence River.

By 1794, Kingston shipped 12,823 bushels of wheat, 896 bushels of flour and 83 barrels of middlings down river to Montreal.

Another 1,624 bushels of wheat and 3,596 barrels of flour were shipped to area garrisons.

Cheese & Pineapple Salad

Presented by Dianne Fisher, Addison

Ingredients:

1 envelope of gelatin   1/4 cup of water
3/4 cup of sugar   1/2 cup of pineapple syrup
1 cup of grated cheese
1 cup (pint) of whipped, whipping cream
1 can of crushed pineapple, drained, save the juice

Method:

Soften the gelatin in cold water. Dissolve the sugar in the pineapple syrup over low heat. Add the softened gelatin, remove from heat and stir, then chill until partially set. Fold in the whipped cream, cheese and crushed pineapple. Chill until set. A mould may be used, if desired.

This recipe can easily be adapted to reflect a lower calorie count by omitting the sugar, using low fat cheese and low fat, powdered, whipped cream substitute.

Dianne Fisher is a nurse who lives in a house called "Moonwinks". She shares her life with two dogs, two cats, two horses, two cows, and one husband, not necessarily in that order. She enjoys gardening and sailing but confesses that she is not really a sailor ... despite her husband's references to walking the plank. Friends rave about her cooking skills.

"Snarlingtown"

Brockville was originally a hamlet called Buell's Bay after William Buell, a United Empire Loyalist. By 1810 it was decided that a courthouse and jail should be built and Buell offered the land.

Buell hoped the hamlet, which then consisted of 26 buildings, would be renamed "Williamstown". Others promoted the name "Charlestown". Cynics, fed up with the bickering that followed, dubbed it "Snarlingtown".

Eventually Buell's Bay was renamed Brockville after Sir Isaac Brock, Upper Canada's new military governor who died in battle during the War of 1812–14.

Largest on the lakes

A 19th century naval arms race coincided with the War of 1812–14 and the British navy produced the largest warship on the Great Lakes – the HMS St. Lawrence.

This behemoth never fired a shot in anger; peace was declared before the St. Lawrence *was launched. Still, she was a formidable vessel manned by 1,000 sailors.*

Her length was 190 feet, her beam was 60 feet and she drew some 23 feet. HMS St. Lawrence *carried 102 guns arranged on two decks.*

The St. Lawrence *made two voyages to Niagara with troops and stores then was turned into a floating barracks at Kingston where she eventually sank.*

Sour Cream Salad

Presented by Dorothy Haesler, Gananoque

Ingredients:

1 cup of boiling water	2 packages of lime Jello
1 pint of whipped sour cream	1 cup of finely chopped nuts
a few drops of green food coloring	
1 small bottle of red maraschino cherries, drained	

Method:

Dissolve the Jello in the boiling water. Let it set until it reaches the consistency of cream then fold in the other ingredients. Pour into a mould to set, then serve.

Dorothy Haesler is an original River Rat born in Rockport on the St. Lawrence where she developed a deep and abiding love for the river. Her culinary skills were sharpened during her employment at one of Gananoque's dining establishments. She has raised a family of four children and, in the process, has acquired a repertoire of stories which she shares with three granddaughters.

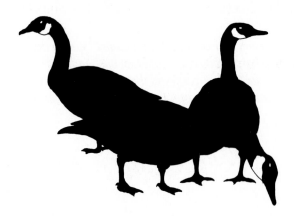

Middle Eastern Coleslaw

Presented by The Village Doctor's Bed & Breakfast
145 Stone Street South, Gananoque

Ingredients for the Coleslaw:

1 green cabbage   2 tbsp of dried mint
1 bunch of chopped green onions   2 tbsp of dried basil
1 red pepper (optional)

Ingredients for the Dressing:

1/4 cup of extra virgin olive oil   2 to 4 minced garlic cloves
1/4 cup fresh or bottled lemon juice salt & fresh ground pepper to taste

Method:

To make this pleasant alternative to summer's creamy salads, slice the cabbage sliver-thin, then cut crossways to make very thin pieces about 1 to 2 inches in length. Place the cabbage in a bowl, preferable one with a snap-on lid. Add the green onion. If you use a red pepper, cut it as you cut the cabbage. Make thin, bite-size slivers then add this to the cabbage and onion. Add the two herbs and mix with your fingers so they are spread evenly through the salad. Depending on the size of your cabbage, you may wish to add or reduce the amount of herbs, but there should be a fair amount throughout the salad.

Measure the oil and lemon juice, add the garlic, salt and pepper and whisk. Pour this over the cabbage mixture and toss, or snap on the bowl's lid and shake. This salad needs to be covered and allowed to marinate at least one hour. It will reduce in volume by about one-third as this happens. A periodic shake or toss during that hour will help blend the flavors.

Laurie Vaughan-Evans and Lee Huddleston operate this delightful bed and breakfast. This decorative building once was the home and office of Dr. W.E. Potter, who arrived here in 1829 to establish Gananoque's first medical practice.

Homemade fizzy pop

This old recipe for root beer comes from a cloth-covered book published early this century and purchased by Ella Spafford. Ella was born in 1892 at Berryton, north of Gananoque, and died in 1982. Today, the book belongs to Ella's daughter, Dora Shields of Lansdowne.

Take 1 oz each of sassafras, allspice, yellow dock and wintergreen, 1/2 oz each of wild cherry bark and coriander, 1/4 oz of hops, 3 qt of molasses. Pour boiling water on the ingredients and let stand for 24 hours. Filter the liquor then add 1/2 pt of yeast and it will be ready for use in 24 hours.

87

Life in the backwoods

Excerpt from Chambers' Edinburgh Journal, *November 21, 1846.*

"... it is the business of the lumberer to penetrate into the primeval forests, and occupy himself during one period of the year in hewing down the trees, which at another period he conveys, by the lakes and river, to the settlements of men. Such an employment, it may be supposed, has no beneficial effect upon the character. Buried among the woods during the entire winter with his desperate comrades, the lumberer has only one task – chopping; and only two amusements – drinking and smoking. When summer comes, and the rivers, loosed from their chains, begin anew to bound, and rush, and roar, he forms his acquisitions into rafts, and the monotonous labours, and equally monotonous pleasures, of winter, are followed by a course of wild and desperate adventure as he plunges down the rapids.

Continued on the next page

Spinach Dip
Presented by Marnie Thomson, Greenbush

Ingredients:

1 large pkg of Knorr vegetable soup	1 cup of sour cream
1 cup of mayonnaise	1 pkg of frozen, chopped spinach
1 pumpernickel bread loaf	

Method:

Thaw the frozen spinach and squeeze out the water. Combine the spinach with the vegetable soup, sour cream and mayonnaise and chill overnight. Before serving, hollow out the pumpernickel loaf and fill with the dip mixture. Serve with pieces of pumpernickel and French bread.

Marnie and Bruce Thomson, their three young children and an assortment of critters of various varieties, live half way between Greenbush and Rocksprings. The Thomsons spend winter weekends dragging stumps, destined to become firewood, from 'the back swamp'. While Marnie, a registered nurse, educates their children at home, Bruce manages the advertising department of Gananoque's weekly newspaper. Bruce is one of those rare people whose presence uplifts the spirits of others ... despite an obsessive attachment to the family's fleet of superannuated Volvos.

Marnie credits her sister-in-law, "who does all things perfectly and does not mind sharing", for this recipe.

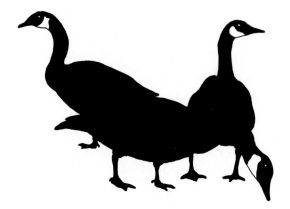

Greek Style Salad

Presented by Aunt Lucy's, 1399 Princess Street, Kingston

Ingredients for the Dressing:

3 tbsp of quality olive oil	1 tbsp of red wine vinegar
1/2 tbsp of lemon juice	1 crushed garlic clove*
1/4 tsp of fresh oregano	salt and pepper to taste

*Rub the bowl with the crushed garlic; leave some in the bowl if you like zest.

Ingredients for the Salad:

tomato wedges	green pepper slices
sliced red onion rings	celery, optional
4 oz crumbled feta cheese to taste	12 kalamata olives
cucumber slices with or without the skin	

Method:

In a salad bowl, assemble the salad ingredients, add the dressing and toss.

Aunt Lucy's has been a Kingston tradition and landmark since 1947. While dining is casual, the food and service are first-rate. Private booths with tapestry upholstered benches, lace curtains, tiffany lamps and stencilled chairs in rose and teal impart a country inn ambiance to the dining room. All dishes are prepared with only the finest and freshest ingredients. Aunt Lucy's is open 7 days a week and is owned by Gerry Warne.

Continued from the previous page

The third phase in his existence is presented by the town, where he drowns the recollection of his toils and dangers in the lowest debauchery, and is perfectly satisfied if his hard-earned dollars last till it is time to betake himself to the woods again."

The Journal also quotes Sir Richard Bonnycastle, a Lieutenant-Colonel in the Royal Engineers and period writer. "A raft a quarter of a mile long ... with its little huts of boards, its apologies for flags and streamers, its numerous little masts and sails, its cooking caboose ... numberless accidents happen: the rafts are broken by storm and tempest; the men get drunk and fall over; and it appears extraordinary that a raft ... should ever reach its destination ... through the ever-agitated fresh-water sea (Lake Ontario—ed.), and amongst the intricate channels of the Thousand Islands.

Monsters of the deep

It wasn't the Loch Ness monster, but Fred Truesdell must have wondered, way back in 1949. He had hooked a 235 pound sturgeon on a night line. The monster was six feet long and one of the largest ever caught in the 1,000 Islands.

Fred's wife made caviar from sturgeon eggs. For every 10 pounds of eggs, she mixed in 1 pound of salt. The mixture was pressed through a screen and when the salt hardened – caviar!

Today, the viability of the lake sturgeon population is tenuous. It was thought they had been eradicated from the 1,000 Islands for two reasons. First, dams interfered with migration to ancestral spawning beds; second, they were over-fished. But a small population was discovered in 1994.

It will take many years for lake sturgeon to re-establish their numbers ... fortunately they can live for as long as 150 years.

New England Clam Chowder
Presented by The Lobster Trap Seafood Restaurant
650 King Street, Gananoque

Ingredients:

1 1/2 cups of diced onions	2 1/2 cups of water*
1/2 cup of butter	5 1/2 tsp of salt
1 tsp of black pepper	2 tbsp of Worcestershire Sauce
1/8 cup of finely chopped celery	1 tbsp of dried parsley
1/4 cup of sugar	2 1/2 cups of cream
5 cups of coarsely diced potatoes	2 cups of fresh clams†
1 finely diced strip of bacon (optional)	

*reserved from boiling the potatoes
†canned clams may be substituted

Method:

Sauté the butter, onion and clams (and bacon if desired) until tender. Boil the potatoes and remove them from the pot, reserving the liquid and adding water to make 2 1/2 cups in the pot. Into this liquid, add the remaining ingredients and bring to a boil. Reduce the heat and add the onions, clams, bacon and boiled potatoes. Simmer until thick and creamy, approximately 3 hours. Top with a pinch of fresh or dried parsley and perhaps a dollop of butter.

The Lobster Trap Seafood Restaurant is owned by the Brown family and is Gananoque's only seafood restaurant. Daily specials include an Early Bird menu. The décor is definitely nautical and includes a large, marine aquarium. A Days Inn franchise shares the property with The Lobster Trap Seafood Restaurant.

Tomato, Sausage and Basil Soup
Presented by The Wellington, 207 Wellington Street, Kingston

Ingredients:

1 large chopped Spanish onion	4 fresh chopped tomatoes
12 cooked breakfast sausages	2 tbsp of basil
2 cups of water	4 cups of tomato juice

Method:

Sauté the onion in olive oil then add the tomatoes and water. Bring to a boil and add the basil and sliced sausages. Simmer until the tomatoes are soft. Add the tomato juice and return to a boil.

Serves 8 to 12.

Editor's Note:

For a memorable repast, this soup goes well with the Wellington's Warm Steak and Pepper Salad...and beer! (See page 46 in the Great Expectations section.)

The Wellington is a pub in the Irish tradition down to dark wood paneling and traditional bar design. Exposed limestone testifies to the heritage nature of the building which once housed a bakery. Today, it offers patrons a choice of tables or cozy booths, a fireplace, darts and pub 'fayre'. Ten beers are on draft; five of them are imported. Manager Peter Schwarz says The Wellington offers some of the finest live music in the city. Monday is blues night; Thursday, jazz; Friday and Saturday nights, Celtic music including performances by Gerry O'Kane, one of the pub's owners; Sunday afternoons feature a live jazz jam and Sunday nights, the Kingston Folk Club. Entertainers range from internationally known to the best of local artists.

Welcome to the garden

To the peoples of the First Nations, the 1,000 Islands region was known as Manatonna, or The Garden of the Great Spirit.

Time, unfortunately, has erased their rock paintings which once were evident at both Landon Bay and at Brockville. A written account exists of the two paintings at Brockville. Each painting represented a canoe containing warriors – five in one and six in the other.

Archaeological digs on the islands have uncovered evidence of the earliest visitors dating back thousands of years. This includes a sharpened rock tool and pottery shards.

Among the other, more recent items discovered were a French gunflint, a King George III penny dated 1775 and a broken clay pipe.

Lured by free land

Recollections of Hiel Sliter, quoted in
History of Leeds and Grenville
1749–1879 by Thaddeus Leavitt.

Mr. Sliter's father was a United Empire Loyalist who visited Upper Canada (Ontario—ed.) to obtain a 200 acre land grant in 1801. He returned home to Vermont and " ... he obtained a yoke of oxen, built a large sleigh, upon which were placed his family and household effects, and with this conveyance started for Canada. The trip occupied nearly five weeks."

The family settled in Leeds County ... "the nearest store was kept by Daniel Jones, where Brockville now stands. The place was known at that time as Snarling-town."

Mr. Jones asked about the Sliters' trip. "This is easier to ask than to answer," responded Mr. Sliter, obviously a master of the understatement.

Cream of Potato Soup

Presented by The Colonial Resort, 780 King Street West, Gananoque

Ingredients:

3 cups of diced potatoes	1 tsp of finely chopped parsley
1 tbsp of butter	6 slices of chopped bacon
2 medium onions	4 tbsp of flour
3 cups of milk	1/8 tsp of paprika
1/3 cup of cream (optional)	salt and pepper to taste

Method:

In a saucepan, cook the diced potatoes with just enough water to cover them. Do not drain.

Leave half of the potatoes in the saucepan with the water; mash the other half of the potatoes and add the chopped parsley. Set this aside.

Melt the butter in a large, heavy pan. Add the chopped bacon and onions and cook gently until soft but not browned. Add flour and cook for 2 minutes. Remove from the heat and whisk in the milk. Return to low heat and cook until smooth and thick, stirring constantly. Add the paprika and whisk again.

Combine both potato mixtures with the cream base described in the foregoing paragraph. Season to taste with salt and pepper. Heat thoroughly. For a richer taste, add cream.

Serves 6.

The Colonial Resort is owned by Jennifer and Bruce Henry and the dining room offers family dining. Bruce and Jennifer were both born and raised in Ireland. They operated two hotels in Scotland before settling in Canada. The Colonial also has an Irish pub. This recipe was submitted by chef Eula Griffin.

Peter Pumpkin Eater's Stuffed Pumpkin Soup

Presented by Mary Joan Barrett, 1,000 Islands Parkway

Ingredients:

6 to 7 lb pumpkin, washed	1 cup of toasted croutons
4 oz of grated Gruyère cheese	salt and pepper to taste
12 cups of chicken stock	1/2 cup of table cream

Method:

Cut a fairly wide lid in the top of the pumpkin. Scoop out the seeds and fibers but save the seeds to roast. Brush a little cooking oil inside on the pumpkin flesh. Set it on an oven-proof serving dish and lay alternate layers of croutons and grated cheese inside the pumpkin. Sprinkle the final layer with salt and pepper and fill with chicken stock, not quite to the top.

Close the 'tureen' with the pumpkin lid as tightly as possible. Place in a 375°F oven and cook for 1 hour, or until the pulp is tender when tested with a fork. Just before serving, stir in the table cream. Serve the soup with scoops of cooked pumpkin.

Serves 8 to 10.

Mary Joan Barrett has filled her life with interesting activities. She has been an importer of wine, she has taught French and German; she is a writer and researcher for historical publications and she collects recipes. It should come as no surprise to learn that she has written a cookbook called In Praise of Pumpkins *containing only pumpkin recipes. This recipe is taken from her book. Recently, Joan has turned her talents to a history of women weavers of the Front of Escott Township.*

A 'bewitching' woman

Jane Barnes is known to this day as The Witch of Plum Hollow, or Mother Barnes, for her uncanny fortune-telling abilities. Plum Hollow is the small, Leeds County village where she lived.

Had she lived in the late 20th century, she probably would have been a television celebrity. Her prognostications once helped authorities find the body of a murder victim and convict the killer.

But most of her fortune-telling was concerned with finding lost articles and predicting future events.

Mother Barnes was born in Ireland in 1794, reportedly the seventh daughter of a seventh daughter, which is supposed to account for her special abilities. She died in 1891 at a ripe old age.

The Abrams Orchestra

By Glenn Abrams

Now is the Hour – *the signature song, and last dance, played many, many times by Bessie Abrams and her Gananoque orchestra. This piece of music, and the one immediately preceding it,* Show Me the Way to Go Home, *wound up many dances all over the district – Gananoque, Inverary, Lansdowne, Wilstead, Elgin, Howe Island, Martin's Barn, Woodburn, Sunbury, Farquharson's Barn and McNeeley's Barn, to name a few locations. The orchestra played in virtually every schoolhouse in the area.*

In the 1930's, Bessie Abrams started entertaining on piano for wedding showers, Christmas concerts, dance recitals and with Harry Campbell's

Continued on the next page

Leek Soup

Presented by Gail Abrams, Brockville

Ingredients:

4 cups of sliced leeks	3 cups of diced potatoes
6 cups of chicken broth	1 cup of whipping cream
salt to taste	3 tbsp of dry vermouth or sherry
chopped chives	

Method:

Cook the leeks and potatoes in a small amount of water. When soft, and after most of the water has evaporated, purée in a blender or food processor. Add this mixture to the chicken broth and heat to boiling. Lower the heat and add the cream then heat the soup to the serving temperature. Add the sherry or vermouth just before serving. Sprinkle with chives and serve either hot or cold.

Makes about 8 to 10 servings of 1 cup each.

Gail Abrams is a business person who has spent nearly a decade in municipal politics. She served nine years on the Brockville City Council and has been in business with husband, Glenn, for 15 years. They operate CIC Coatings. Originally from Lansdowne, Gail follows her mother, Abbie Nunn's example, as an excellent cook. Glenn shares his memories of his mother's orchestra on this and the following page.

Cream of Mushroom Soup with Horseradish

Presented by Chez Piggy Restaurant, 68-R Princess Street, Kingston

Ingredients:

1 1/2 quarts of chicken stock	1 cup of white wine
1 medium potato cut into quarters	1 tbsp of dried porcini mushrooms
1 diced onion	1 diced celery stalk
3 garlic cloves, chopped	3/4 lb of sliced mushrooms
3 tbsp of butter	2 cups of whipping cream
3 tbsp of prepared horseradish	salt and pepper to taste

Method:

Mix the stock and wine in a large pot then add the potato pieces and simmer until the potato is cooked. Remove the potato and mash it and return to the stock. Now add the porcini mushrooms to the stock.

In a frying pan, sauté the onion, celery and garlic with 1 tbsp of butter. When the vegetables are transparent, add them to the stock. Using the same frying pan, cook the mushrooms in two separate batches, each with 1 tbsp of butter. (You may fry them in one batch if your frying pan is large enough). Cook the mushrooms on high heat, stirring frequently so that the liquid will evaporate and the mushrooms have a nice brown color. Add the cooked mushrooms to the stock.

In a separate pan, reduce the cream by 1/3 and remove from the heat. Stir the horseradish into the cream and add the cream mixture to the stock. Season with salt and pepper and your soup is ready to serve 4 to 6 people.

Chez Piggy offers imaginative, international cuisine complemented by an extensive wine list. All desserts and breads are baked daily at its bakery, Pan Chancho, 70 Johnson Street. Many of Chez Piggy's desserts and other menu items are available there for take-out as well as a wide selection of salads, patés and imported cheeses. The chef is Victoria Newbury; co-owners are Rose Richardson and Zal Yanovsky.

Continued from the previous page
"Troupe". During the war, the Troupe entertained the forces at several locations.

She organized an orchestra from these beginnings with such great backup people as Roy and "Hammy" Hampton, Leo Slack, Claude Andrews, Sam Seaman, Bill Tyson, Bill La Sha, Keith Clow and many others. At different periods of time, daughter Betty (now Betty Higgins of the Gananoque area—ed.) sat in on drums and son Glenn (the author of this piece—ed.) joined on trumpet.

Mrs. Abrams had the enviable ability to pick up and play a song 'by ear' and to transpose into any key suitable to the other members, or a vocalist.

The Abrams Orchestra played dances until the late '50's and will be remembered by many for its delivery of the old standards and square dance music.

A runaway slave

Excerpts from Chambers's Edinburgh Journal, *1847.*

"While meditating one Sabbath evening, a few weeks ago, upon the blessings of this free, gospel land, and on the liberty wherewith God here sets his children free, a neighbour opened the door, and whispered cautiously in our ear that a young sable fugitive from slavery had knocked at his door ... there were many of us that gathered around that young man, and few of us all had ever seen a slave ... He was chequered over with the marks of the scourge for his master had prescribed a hundred lashes to cure him of his passion for freedom ... A worse fate awaited him if he failed in his third attempt ... He walked to the window, and softly asked the nearest way to Canada. 'Canada and Heaven,' he said, 'were the only two places that the slave sighed for,' and he tied up his clouted shoes to go."

Grill Tomato Soup

Presented by The Clarence Street Grill, 6 Clarence Street, Kingston

Ingredients:

1 tbsp of olive oil
1 red onion, finely chopped
2 tbsp of tomato paste
pinch of cayenne
1 roasted red pepper, skin removed, sliced
2 to 3 cups of chicken broth, home-made or canned
1 can (16 oz) of plum tomatoes with juice, use fresh tomatoes in season

1/2 to 1 tbsp of fresh minced garlic
1 to 2 oz of balsamic vinegar
mixture of basil, thyme, oregano
pinch of salt

Method:

Sauté the garlic and onions in olive oil until soft. Purée the tomatoes and red pepper in a food processor or blender. Add the juice from the tomato can and process further. Place this mixture in a large (non-reactive) pot with the onions and garlic. Add the chicken broth and spices and simmer over medium-low heat for an hour.

Remove from the heat and add the balsamic vinegar, salt and pepper to taste. Garnish with a dollop of sour cream or yogurt and a watercress sprig or fresh basil leaf.

Serves 4.

This is their famous signature recipe which is very popular with patrons of The Clarence Street Grill. It is owned by Leslie Leacy and Mark Smith and specializes in nouvelle cuisine. *Sunday brunch, lunches and dinners are served. In season, enjoy the view of Kingston's harbor from an outdoor patio. Art posters, plants and flaming pink flamingoes create an atmosphere of casual elegance. Reasonable prices.*

Great Conclusions

Elderberry Pie
Presented by Martha Landon, Lansdowne

Ingredients:

4 cups of fresh elderberries	1 cup of sugar
3 tbsp of all purpose flour	1/2 tsp of grated lemon peel
1/2 tsp of ground cinnamon*	dash of salt
pastry for two double 9" pies	1 tsp of lemon juice
1 tbsp of butter	

*nutmeg may be substituted

Method:

Combine the elderberries with the sugar, flour, lemon peel and cinnamon (or nutmeg) and add a dash of salt. Line two 9" pie plates with pastry and fill with the elderberry mixture. Sprinkle with the lemon juice and dot with the butter. Adjust the top crusts and cut slits for steam to escape. Seal the crusts and bake the pies at 400°F for 35 to 40 minutes. Serve warm if desired.

Martha, and her husband Byron, live on a dairy farm near the village of Lansdowne. During their courtship, Byron asked Martha to make his favorite dessert, elderberry pie. He even provided some fresh elderberries. "Obviously this is a test," Martha thought to herself as she accepted the berries and the challenge, although she had never cooked an elderberry pie. So she improvised and based this recipe on her blueberry pie formula. It worked. Byron was pleased with the pie and The Question was popped. Martha accepted and they live happily ever after.

But there is more. Shortly after marriage, Martha decided to reprise her elderberry pie success. For reasons unknown, the second batch of pies failed. Miserably and then some. Isn't fate fickle? Suppose the first batch had failed? Regardless, this is the elderberry pie recipe which contributed to a great match.

Byron is the fifth generation Landon to farm the property which has been in the family since 1831.

Bucks for bangs

Byron Landon's grandfather earned extra money by removing stones from neighbors' fields. He used two methods: the quiet way was to use a stone puller, a contraption involving a wheel and some chain; the second method was noisier.

Byron's grandfather packed blasting powder on top of a rock and weighed it down with other stones and earth. This was called a mud shot. A family account book records a profitable day in 1888 when 28 stones were pulled or blasted at 25 cents each for a total of $7.50.

99

Pioneer commodities

Thomas Darling and his family operated 19th century commercial enterprises along the St. Lawrence River and in the village of Lansdowne. Here is a partial store inventory from 1858.

Gingham, lace, dishes, carriage leather and whips, baking powder, castor oil, boot blacking, various ribbons, buttons, pins, bolts of cloth, candlesticks, hardware, door locks, springs, hammers, school books, bibles, copy books, lead pencils, thread, brooms, rakes, saltpeter, starch, alum, pepper, shaving soap, cornstarch, green coffee, sugar, indigo, tea, cloves, herring and codfish.

It is revealing that no alcohol products are mentioned. A dozen miles to the west, there were no such inhibitions in Gananoque. Ten years earlier, in 1848, 3,086 gallons of alcohol were bought and sold for £480 9s, also 3,924 gallons of malt liquor and cider at £145 10s.

White Caps Cake
Presented by Ivy Lea Resort & Marina, Ivy Lea

Ingredients for the Cake:

2 cups of flour	2 tsp of baking soda
2 cups of sugar	2 eggs
1 large can of pineapple tidbits	

Ingredients for the Icing:

1 cup of grated cocoanut	1 cup of sugar
1/4 lb of butter	1 can of evaporated milk

Method for the Cake:

Preheat the oven to 350°F. Mix the flour and baking soda and set aside. In a separate bowl, beat the eggs and sugar together until fluffy. Add the pineapple and flour and soda mixture. Stir just until mixed. Pour the batter into a prepared 12" round pan. Bake for 30 to 40 minutes until set and browned on top. Ice while the cake is warm.

Method for the Icing:

On the stovetop, bring the sugar, butter and milk to a boil for 3 minutes, stirring constantly. Remove from the heat and add the cocoanut. Pour the hot icing mixture over the warm cake.

Under new management, the Ivy Lea Resort & Marina is located in the heart of the 1,000 Islands. The dining room seats 75 comfortably and provides a riverside view of dramatic sunsets common in this area. An outdoor patio seats another 75. Canadian cuisine is featured and reservations are recommended on weekends and during the summer months. The resort presides over 35 acres in a spectacular, natural setting and includes a large marina.

Pauline's Bonny Wee Trifle

Presented by Pauline Caldwell, Gananoque

Ingredients:

2 packages of regular Jello	fruit (see below)
6 ladyfingers	sherry to taste
custard powder	whipped cream, mid-sized carton
sprinkles	3 tbsp of sugar

Method:

When making trifle, any combination of Jello and fruit may be used; just match the flavors. If you make a sherry trifle, use strawberries. Sherry is optional but remember, if it is used, you must reduce the amount of water in the Jello to equal the quantity of sherry. This applies as well to juice from tinned fruit. If there is too much liquid, the Jello will not set.

The dish used for this recipe is round, about 10" in diameter and 4" in depth. Mix the Jello with water as directed on the package. Add fresh or tinned fruit and 6 ladyfingers, which may be set in the dish whole or crumbled, then place in the refrigerator to set.

Make the custard by following the directions on the tin; for a large trifle, double the quantities. Let it cool then pour on top of the set Jello. Return this to the refrigerator. Make sweetened whipped cream by adding the sugar then spread on top of the custard then top with multi-colored sprinkles.

For a smaller trifle, halve all ingredients.

Pauline Caldwell is a Scottish lassie, originally from Edinburgh, who lives in Gananoque. A word of warning: her trifle may be addictive. This dish is so good that at the very least it should be illegal ... which thankfully it isn't.

Colder in the colonies

Excerpts from Chambers's Edinburgh Journal, *December, 1846, reviewing* The Emigrant *by Sir Francis B. Head, Bart.*

"Speaking of the grandeur of the works of nature in America, he (Sir Francis—ed) observes that 'the heavens are infinitely higher – the sky bluer – the clouds are whiter – the air is fresher – the cold is intenser – the moon looks larger – the stars are brighter – the thunder is louder – the lightning is vivider – the wind is stronger – the rain is heavier – the mountains are higher – the rivers larger – the forests bigger – the plains broader' ...

"Of the intensity of the Canadian cold no one in Britain can have the slightest conception ... If not thoroughly protected by furs, the blood chills; and according to Sir Francis, the frost-bitten fingers and toes can be broken off like twigs ... ice is much harder and colder than English ice."

Butter your axles

Brockville, which once rejoiced to the derisive label, Snarlingtown, became a self-governing village in 1832. While some of its residents may have enjoyed conflict, the area's farmers were earning a reputation for butter although most Ontario butter of that era was dismissed as 'axle grease'.

Brockville area butter was rich and sweet and became a local specialty. It sold well in the United States and by 1865 Brockville butter was well known in England where it was sold well into the 1880's.

Today, Brockville residents are proud that theirs is the oldest incorporated municipality in Ontario. The city has 21,000 residents and the Snarlingtown designation has been consigned to history's scrap heap.

Marmalade Fruit Cake
Presented by Laura Boszormeny, Brockville

Ingredients:

2 cups of butter (1 lb)
2 cups of demerara sugar
4 eggs
2 shots of dark rum*
1/2 cup of citron peel
1/2 cup of undiluted frozen orange juice
1 lb of halved red and green cherries (2 cups)
2 tangy marmalades, 1 imported (1 cup) and 1 domestic (2 cups)

7 cups of all purpose flour
4 tsp of baking powder
2 cups of currants
2 cups of raisins

*Demerara Fruit-Cured Rum is best

Method:

Sift the flour and baking powder in a large bowl. Add the prepared fruit and dredge. Cream the butter in a large bowl or dishpan and gradually add the brown sugar. Add the beaten eggs, then rum, orange juice and marmalades. Now, add the fruit mixture and mix well; use your hands if necessary.

Bake in greased, lined pans at 300°F for about 2 hours. Place a tin of water in the oven during baking. Test the cake with a cake tester after 2 hours and remove from the oven when the tester comes out clean. Let the cakes cool in the pans, then on a wire rack. Wrap the cakes in rum-soaked cheese cloth, waxed paper and tinfoil. Allow to mellow on a dark shelf for a week before freezing.

Makes about 5 cakes, depending on pan size.

Laura was born in Ontario and raised in Quebec. In 1974, she and her husband returned to her roots and bought some rural property outside Brockville. Laura has taught elementary school and is a "happy hooker" of the rug variety. Traditional hooked rugs are her specialty. She has raised a team of sled dogs, with her husband, Les, and is raising a pair of sons. Her idea of purgatory involves obedience classes with a disinterested Siberian Husky.

Yankee Pancakes

Presented by Pat Lackie, Lansdowne

Ingredients for the Pancakes:

1 cup of sour milk*

1 tsp of salt

1 tsp of soda

1 cup of flour

*Add a small amount of vinegar to the milk to turn it sour

Ingredients for the Sauce:

1 quart of hot water

lemon or nutmeg

small amount of vinegar

corn starch

1/2 cup of brown sugar

Method:

Combine the pancake ingredients. Roll this mixture flat with a rolling pin then cut the pancakes to whatever size you prefer. Fry them as you would a fried cake.

Add the sauce ingredients to the hot water and mix. Pour the sauce over the hot pancakes for a delicious treat.

Lansdowne's Pat Lackie cooked at Gananoque's Provincial Motel for 10 years. This recipe was given to her by her mother, the late Edith Griffin. Her parents raised 13 children who crossed Gananoque Lake by boat or walked across the frozen ice to attend school. Pat is not sure how long this recipe has been a family favorite.

A swinish situation

Back in 1918, Robert Webster's father hired a pair of carpenters for the summer. There was much for them to do on the Lansdowne area farm.

Come time to settle up, Robert's father decided to pack a pig off to nearby Mallorytown to raise money to pay the debt. Well, the prize porker proved to be worth more than the combined wages of the carpenters.

Clutching their earnings, they decamped muttering that it was a sorry day when a pig's value exceeded that of the labor of two carpenters.

103

Send the gunboats!

Today, the 1,000 Islands is a peaceful playground straddling the world's longest, undefended border. But from 1812 until Christmas Eve of 1814, Canada and the United States were caught up in an unpopular war and the islands echoed to the thunder of naval gunfire.

The war's workhorses were gunboats, wide, shallow-drafted, single decked vessels without cabins. These highly maneuverable floating gun platforms were used extensively for in-shore support of landings, to bombard military installations and for scouting and convoy work amidst the islands.

Sweeps, or oars, thrust through holes in the bulwarks created the appearance of multi-legged insects. Indeed, American Commodore Chanucey's squadron was known as 'Chauncey's Water Spiders'.

Continued on the next page

White Chocolate Raspberry Mousse Cake

Presented by Peck's Marina & Restaurant, 1,000 Islands Parkway

Ingredients for the White Chocolate Mousse:

1 lb of white chocolate   3 cups of 35% cream

Ingredients for the Pastry Crust:

2 cups of butter   4 1/2 cups of flour
1 1/4 cups of sugar

Ingredients for the Raspberry Mousse:

1 envelope of unflavored gelatin   2 tbsp of cold water
1 tbsp of lemon juice   2 egg whites
3 cups of frozen raspberries (thawed)   1 cup of sugar

Method:

Prepare the white chocolate mousse the day before by melting the chocolate. Scald the cream and add to the melted chocolate then refrigerate overnight.

The crust should also be prepared the day before. Place the ingredients in the food processor and process until crumbly, approximately 20 seconds. Press the mixture into a lightly greased 10" spring form pan. Prick it with a fork then bake blind until light golden brown at 420°F. Leave it in the spring form pan.

Continued on the next page

Continued from the previous page

To assemble, prepare the raspberry mousse by combining the gelatin and water in a small saucepan. Soak for 5 minutes. Stir in the raspberries, reserving 1/2 cup, and add the lemon juice. Bring gently to a boil, stirring frequently then set aside to cool to room temperature.

Make a meringue by very slowly adding the sugar to the egg whites as they are beaten to form soft peaks. Fold the berry mixture into the meringue adding the reserved berries.

Whip the white chocolate mixture to the consistency of a thick cream. Scoop the white chocolate mousse into the pastry crust which is still in the spring form. Coat the bottom and sides generously with the mousse. Now, scoop the raspberry mousse into the chocolate mousse lined crust to fill the center. Drop any remaining white chocolate mousse into the center in dabs and marble with raspberry mousse.

Refrigerate for 6 hours before serving. Serves 14.

This recipe is presented by Don and Kate Hunter who operate Peck's Marina and Restaurant. Located on the shore of the St. Lawrence River, this is a delightful place to visit by car or boat. Don is an accomplished chef who specializes in pastries. The atmosphere here is casual, relaxed and the vista of the river activity and islands is spectacular.

Continued from the previous page

Early gunboats were armed with six pounder cannons. By war's end, they mounted 18 or 24 pounder long guns, which were 12 to 15 feet in length, and 32 pounder carronades. These were called 'smashers' because of their destructive power.

If their firepower was awesome for their size (40 to 60 feet), so too were their warlike names. Here is a sampling from British records: Axeman, Blazer, Blisterer, Belabourer, Bloodletter, Boxer, Caustic, Chopper, Crippler, Surprise, Blacksnake and Cleopatra ... *one wonders how the 'Cleo' fit in with such a pugilistic lot.*

A gunboat crew of 38 included sailors, militiamen and gunners from artillery regiments. An equal number of soldiers provided manpower for landings or boardings.

105

Challenged to learn

Excerpts from History of Leeds and Grenville 1749–1879 *by Thaddeus Leavitt.*

"Mr. Sliter's opportunities for obtaining an education were of the most meagre character. He did not attend school until after he was fifteen years of age and then only one month, to learn to write. No regular school was held. Those anxious to learn met at the settler's cabin in the evening, selected the best qualified as teacher and proceeded to business."

And this recollection of Hiel Sliter, mentioned above, reported by Leavitt:

" 'In September, 1812, I joined a rifle company and entered upon duty at Gananoque. While in charge of the Block House, at that place, I learned the multiplication table. As no slates were to be had, my companion and myself obtained some chalk, and by using the top of the stove as a slate, succeeded in mastering the simple rules of arithmetic'."

Grandma's Molasses Cookies

Presented by Yolande LaPointe, Lansdowne

Ingredients:

1 cup of sugar	3/4 cup of melted shortening
1 cup of molasses	1 egg
1 tsp of salt	1 tsp of ginger
1 tsp of cloves	1/2 cup of boiling coffee*
3 tsp of soda	5 cups of flour

*The coffee is made up of 1 tbsp of instant coffee in boiling water. Allow it to cool before using.

Method:

Melt the shortening, add the sugar and mix well. Add the molasses and egg and mix again. Dissolve the soda in the cooled coffee. In a separate bowl, mix the dry ingredients with 2 cups of flour. Add the liquid and mix in the remaining flour except for 1/2 cup which should be reserved for the rolling board.

Roll the dough to 1/4" thickness and cut with a medium sized glass dipped in flour. Cook at 350°F for 10 to 12 minutes.

Yolande LaPointe is the librarian at Front of Leeds and Lansdowne Township Public Library in Lansdowne. Her husband is retired from the Canadian armed forces. This recipe is an old favorite of the Lapointe family. Yolande says it has been passed on from generation to generation of LaPointe Acadian ancestors in New Brunswick.

Rice Pudding

Presented by The Colonial Resort, 780 King Street West, Gananoque

Ingredients:

1 cup of uncooked rice
3/4 cup of sugar
2 tsp of vanilla
nutmeg to taste
3 cups of whipped cream (optional)

8 cups of milk
pinch of salt
2 tsp of cinnamon
3/4 cup of seedless raisins

Method:

Wash the raisins then soak them in warm water. Wash the rice then combine the rice with the milk and add salt. Place the mixture in a double boiler and simmer gently until the rice is cooked and the mixture is thick and creamy. Stir often.

Remove from the heat and add the raisins, nutmeg, cinnamon, sugar and vanilla. Cool then add the whipped cream, if desired, and blend.

Serves 8 to 10.

The Colonial Resort is owned by Jennifer and Bruce Henry. The Colonial's dining room offers family dining. Bruce and Jennifer were both born and raised in Ireland. They operated two hotels in Scotland before settling in Canada. The Colonial also has an Irish pub. This recipe was submitted by chef Romeo Bonucchi who has earned local fame for his chili. Alas — he will not part with that recipe.

The cheese board

Early in this century, a 'cheese board' met in Lansdowne every Monday. Its members supervised the bidders gathered to buy the large cheese wheels which had been graded at individual cheese factories on the previous Friday.

The Saturday after the cheese board meeting, farmers who supplied the cheese factories with milk, shifted the cheese stocks to Lansdowne's railway station for shipping. Ralph Smith as a youngster remembers horse-drawn wagon loads of cheese creaking past his laneway. There was no refrigeration then, around 1920, and he recalls oil from the cheddar oozing from the wagon boxes.

Although some excellent cheese was produced, Ralph recalls that "there was some awful putrid stuff called cheese back in those days".

A $50 building lot

Gananoque was growing in 1824 so it was surveyed and streets were laid out. A 60 by 120 foot building lot on Main Street cost $50.

A ship-building industry began in 1832 with the construction of the Iroquois *which was designed to shoot rapids. By the 1850's, Gananoque was compared to the heavily industrialized English city of Birmingham. The power of the Gananoque River turned the wheels of industry.*

In 1849, the village consisted of 125 families totaling 768 residents, 316 were fathers and sons; 312 were mothers and daughters. There were 38 male servants, 47 female servants, 46 male boarders and 9 female boarders.

Cooper Family Pumpkin Cheesecake
Presented by Veronica Cooper, Gananoque

Crust Ingredients:
1 1/2 cups of crushed graham crackers or ginger snaps

2 tbsp of sugar   1/3 cup of unsalted butter, melted

Filling Ingredients:
2 pkg (8 oz each) light cream cheese   2 cups of pumpkin purée

1/2 cup of brown sugar   1/2 cup of white sugar

2 tbsp of all purpose flour   1 tsp of vanilla extract

4 eggs   1/4 tsp of mace

1/2 tsp each of cinnamon, ginger, cloves

Method:
Preheat the oven to 350°F. Melt the butter in a medium saucepan then add cookie crumbs and sugar. Combine well. Butter the bottom and sides of an 8" springform pan and distribute the crumbs evenly on the bottom. Bake for 8 to 10 minutes and allow it to cool to room temperature.

Again, preheat the oven to 350°F. Break up the softened cream cheese with a fork then blend in the pumpkin, sugars, flour, spices, vanilla and salt. You can use an electric mixer for this. Beat in the eggs one at a time until the mixture is smooth and creamy. Pour into the crust and bake for one hour or until a toothpick inserted in the center comes out clean. Chill for at least 1 hour; it is better if chilled overnight. Then remove from the pan to a serving plate. Serve with your choice of whipped cream, ginger-snap crumbs or chocolate curls.

Veronica Cooper is a freelance writer and mother of three. Her life's ambition is "to be Erma Bombeck when I grow up". She created this recipe after her family grew enough pumpkins to feed a small country. "We puréed, we pickled, we baked and broiled and still couldn't use them up!" The editors enjoyed especially her ingenuity in disposing of the last pumpkin. She shipped it, COD, to an unsuspecting brother in Calgary.

Snowdrops

Presented by Katherine Warren, Gananoque

Editors' Note:

We have included some of these easy cookies and squares because they are fun to make with children. Half the fun is in the names. See Snicker Doodles, Molasses Moons, Hello Dollies, Sunbeams, Sand Hearts and Lazy Squares, elsewhere in this section.

Ingredients:

2 eggs whites	1/2 tsp of salt
1/2 tsp of vanilla or almond flavoring	1 cup of sifted icing sugar
1/2 cup of rolled oats	candied cherry halves
1/3 cup of chopped, candied cherries	1 cup of flaked/shredded cocoanut

Method:

Preheat the oven to 300°F. Beat the egg whites and salt until the mixture is stiff. Add the flavoring then the sugar, a tablespoon at a time, beating constantly until the mixture is stiff and glassy. Gently fold in the oats, 1/3 cup of candied cherries and cocoanut. Drop from a teaspoon onto a greased cookie sheet. Place a candied cherry half on each mound. Bake for 30 to 35 minutes.

Katherine Warren's mother, the late Margaret Crouch, collected recipes for many years and loved to cook.

Hard time – bad food

Excerpts from Rules and Regulations of the Penitentiary, *for Kingston Penitentiary, 1836.*

"All convicts, as the law enjoins, shall be supplied with a sufficient quantity of inferior, but wholesome, food. Rations, both as it respects quantity and quality, to be regulated, from time to time, by the Inspectors ... The Steward shall be careful to manage the food of the convicts to the best advantage, and vary the cooking so far as may be practicable."

No one could accuse authorities of spoiling the prisoners. The diet table, published October 1, 1836, repeats the same foods over a seven day period – bread, fresh beef, potatoes, coffee, molasses, soup, salt beef, soup, porridge and salt pork. There is no reference to vegetables or fruit, not even 'inferior but wholesome'. If hard time didn't break the spirit, the diet did.

109

No room at the inn?

Excerpt from Cornhill Magazine, *1862,
an anonymously written article entitled*
The Winter in Canada.

*"Ordinary winter life in Canada is not
subject to Arctic severity or dangerous
exposure: it is, on the contrary, the most
healthful season of the year – dry, brac-
ing and cheerful; but the resources of
Quebec, Montreal, Kingston, Toronto,
Niagara and London – the towns in
which barracks are to be found – will
be severely taxed to find accommoda-
tion, and, at first, it is not unlikely that
we may hear of some minor inconve-
niences in consequence of the cram."*

Crêpe Suzette for Four
Presented by The General Wolfe Hotel, Wolfe Island

Ingredients for the Crêpe Mixture (2 per serving):

1/2 cup of half & half cream

4 oz of all purpose flour

pinch of salt

vegetable oil for greasing the pan

2 eggs

grated lemon peel from 1/2 lemon

1/2 oz of brandy

Ingredients for the Sauce:

2 tbsp of butter

2 lemon halves

juice from 1 lemon

2 tbsp of Grand Marnier

8 scoops of vanilla ice cream

8 tbsp of granulated sugar

2 orange halves

2 tbsp of toasted almonds

2 tbsp of brandy

Method:

Mix the crêpe ingredients well, strain off and pour paper-thin pancakes into a 6"
pan well greased with the oil. Cook both sides until they look dry.

Heat a heavy-bottomed skillet over a 350°F oven. Arrange a ring of sugar then
place the butter in the center and cook until the mixture starts to caramelize. Do
not allow it to turn brown. Flame with the brandy, add lemon juice and fruit
halves, cut sides down. Rub the fruit against the pan bottom to free it from sticking and to release its juices. Simmer until the sauce separates behind the spoon,
remove the fruit.

Put the crêpes in the sauce, one at a time. Fold each side in toward the center
then flame with the Grand Marnier. Sprinkle with toasted almonds and serve
flaming over two scoops of vanilla ice cream.

*Miro and Hana Zborovsky own and operate this 135 year old hotel which is reached by a 20-
minute ferry ride to Wolfe Island.*

Swedish Tea Rings

Presented by Viola Griffin, Marble Rock

Ingredients:

1 cup of butter or shortening
2 eggs, separated
walnuts, finely chopped

1/2 cup of brown sugar
2 cups of flour

Method:

Cream the butter or shortening and brown sugar. Add two egg yolks and blend in the flour. Shape into small balls; dip in slightly beaten egg whites then roll in the finely chopped walnuts.

Place the balls on a greased cookie sheet and press a hollow in the center of each. Bake at 350°F for 5 minutes, remove and press centers again. Return to the oven for another 15 minutes. Remove from oven and while hot, fill the centers with jam or jelly.

Viola credits her mother-in-law, Mae Griffin, with this recipe. It is a favorite at the Griffin house, especially when daughter Linda, grandchildren and great-grandchildren visit.

The first residents

Excerpts from Grenadier Island, Steps Through Time, *part of the* Heritage Highlights *series published by St. Lawrence Islands National Park in 1990.*

"From French accounts, we learn that in the early 1600's, the Iroquois were living here year-round in villages, growing corn, and supplementing their diet with fish and game. Tonionta, a large Iroquois village, was referred to on early maps and by Jesuits in their journals ... The Iroquois chose to live on the river, probably on Grenadier Island, so that they could maintain strategic control over their enemies, the Huron. However, the exact location of Tonionta remains a mystery today. Later, by the 1600's the French became their enemies, and the Iroquois effectively prevented them from using the St. Lawrence River, forcing French fur traders to follow the northern Ottawa River route ... By 1650 however, the Iroquois had left the area in great numbers ..."

111

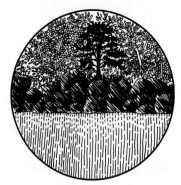

Chocolate Elegance Cookies

Presented by The Sleepless Goat Café, 91 Princess Street, Kingston

Ingredients for Cookies:

1 1/4 cups of unsalted butter	2 cups of all purpose flour, unsifted
2 cups of sugar	3/4 cup of cocoa
2 eggs	1 tsp of baking powder
2 tsp of vanilla	1/2 tsp of salt

Ingredients for Glaze:

6 oz of the finest quality semisweet chocolate (1 square = 1 oz)

4 oz of unsweetened butter	1 tbsp of corn syrup

Method:

Cream the butter and sugar in a large bowl. Add the eggs and vanilla and blend well. Combine the flour, cocoa, baking powder and salt; blend into the creamed mixture and refrigerate for 30 minutes.

Roll the dough into 1 1/2" balls using your hands, then place them on a baking sheet lined with parchment. Sprinkle with sugar then press them to 1/8" thickness using a flat-bottomed glass or bowl. Bake at 350°F for 8 or 9 minutes, just until firm. Do not over bake. Cool on the sheet.

Next, melt together the chocolate, butter and corn syrup in the top of a double boiler over barely simmering water. Carefully glaze each cookie and store in an air-tight container at room temperature.

The Sleepless Goat Café is a coffee house which specializes in homemade food with no additives. Specialty coffees, bistro-style crêpes, pasta, quickie salads and homemade desserts are featured. The atmosphere is modern and upbeat and a local artist creates blackboard menus which are works of art in themselves. The name is based on an Ethiopian legend about a shepherd and his goat. The goat discovered some unfamiliar berries and ate what turned out to be coffee beans ... voila! A Sleepless Goat. The café's general manager is Sodi Hundal and the pastry chef, who provided the recipe, is Renée Comesotti.

Buttermilk Doughnuts

Presented by Beatrice Webster, Lansdowne

Ingredients:

2 eggs
1/4 cup of cooking oil
4 cups of all purpose flour
3/4 tsp of salt
1 cup of buttermilk
1 lb of shortening

1 cup of granulated sugar
1 tsp of vanilla
4 tsp of baking powder
1/4 tsp of baking soda
1 lb of lard

Method:

Beat the eggs until they are thick and lemon colored. Add the sugar and beat until this mixture is smooth. Stir in the cooking oil and vanilla. Blend the dry ingredients and add to the egg mixture, alternating with the buttermilk. Turn this mixture onto a lightly floured surface and roll the dough to 1/2 inch thickness. Cut with a floured doughnut cutter.

Beatrice uses 1 lb of lard and 1 lb of shortening for her cooking oil mixture. Fry in deep, hot fat (375°F) until the doughnuts are golden brown, about 3 minutes. Turn and brown the other side but turn once only. Drain on layers of newspaper which have been covered with paper towel.

Serve plain or sprinkled with sugar. Makes 2 dozen.

This cooking oil mixture can be used many times. Let it cool, pour into a container and refrigerate for further use. Add another pound of shortening or lard.

Beatrice Webster can trace her family (the McCready's) to 1793, when they came to Canada. She lives with her husband, Robert, on their farm where they manage the oldest, registered Holstein herd in Leeds County.

Stop or I'll shoot!

Robert Webster, Beatrice's husband, can trace his ancestry all the way back to Ireland in 1788 when his great, great-grandfather, also named Robert, was born. He was one of 19 children, nine of them emigrated to Canada.

Robert the Irish emigrant had a son named John who married a small woman named Fanny Foley who smoked a pipe. A bear had the nerve to attack one of Fanny's sheep but she had the last word in the matter – she shot the bear.

John and Fanny built the family homestead, and started the farm which has been in the family since 1853. They began with a log cabin and a bearskin over the door (no one is sure whether it was Fanny's bear).

When they needed flour, John walked 30-odd miles to Kingston bearing a sack of wheat to be ground into flour. Then he walked home again.

Measuring distances

The French, the first Europeans to ply the waters of the St. Lawrence River in the 15th and 16th centuries, planted poplar trees along its banks. These marked stopping places selected by the first voyageurs.

Interestingly, the voyageurs measured distance by the number of pipesfull of tobacco which could be smoked between one point and another, hence a distance was measured in 'pipes' as in "The next stop is six pipes away".

Supplies and men were shifted from Montreal to Kingston – Fort Frontenac at Cataraqui, in those days – using Algonkian-made canoes of birch bark. The name Cataraqui is said to mean "a bank of clay rising out of the waters".

"Depending upon the current relations with the Indians and the English, the route was either safe, mildly exciting or very dangerous," according to the authors of a local history.

Chocolate Grand Marnier Ice Cream Cake

Presented by The River Mill Restaurant, 2 Cataraqui Street, Kingston

Ingredients for the Cake:

3 oz of butter	1 cup of sugar
1 splash of vanilla extract	1 large egg
1 cup of flour	1/2 cup of cocoa
pinch of salt	1/2 tsp of baking powder
2/3 cup of water	

Ingredients for Ice Cream:

1/2 cup of sugar	6 egg yolks
2 cups (1/2 liter) of 18% cream	1/3 cup of chocolate syrup
1 1/2 oz of Grand Marnier	

Method:

To make the cake, mix with a beater the butter and sugar then add the vanilla and eggs and mix again. Add the remaining cake ingredients and mix then place the mixture in an 8" greased and floured round pan. Bake at 350°F for 35 minutes. Remove the cake from the pan and allow to cool then slice the cake in half and place the bottom half back in the cake pan.

To create the ice cream mixture, combine the sugar and egg yolks in a double boiler. Whisk until creamy and slightly thick. Remove from heat. Scald the cream and add to the egg mixture then whisk in the remaining ingredients. Freeze in an ice cream machine. Apply the ice cream mixture over the layer of cake still in the pan then add the cake's top layer. Freeze for 1 hour then remove from the pan. Slice and garnish with berries and cream.

The River Mill Restaurant is owned and operated by Colin Altimas and Mark Kennedy. Chef Gary Appleton submitted this recipe.

Sunbeams

Presented by Abbie Nunn, Brockville

Ingredients:

2 egg whites, stiffly beaten
1/2 tsp of baking powder
1 cup of walnuts
Rice Krispies

1 cup of white sugar
1 cup of cocoanut
1/2 lb of dates, finely chopped

Method:

Sift together the sugar and baking powder then fold this mixture into the beaten egg whites. In a separate bowl, mix the cocoanut, nuts and dates then combine them with the first mixture and roll in Rice Krispies.

Bake at 375°F for 10 or 12 minutes.

Abbie Nunn and her late husband, Clifford, owned and operated the Lansdowne Food Lockers from 1947 to 1965. When purchased, it was a typical country general store. By 1952 they had transformed it into a modern, self-serve grocery store and locker plant. The store built its reputation on quality meats and service. Abbie remained in Lansdowne until 1991 when she moved to Brockville. Today the store is called Lansdowne Fresh Mart and it is owned and operated by Abbie's grandsons, Silvan and Yulrick Fernetich.

Wheels of progress

Thaddeus Leavitt in the History of Leeds and Grenville 1749–1879 *writes about an early wheeled vehicle made by "sawing the wheels from the end of a very large log, putting an axle in, and building a rough box above". That Leavitt was a wit as well as an historian is evident from his next remark.*

"No doubt, on such state occasions as a wedding, this unique vehicle was in request for the bridal tour."

Leavitt mentions an 1837 stage coach which passed through Brockville. Calling it "a heavy, lumbering vehicle, reeling and tumbling along; pitching like a scow", he estimates its speed at two miles per hour. We're not sure whether he was being facetious, but he does qualify the observation by relating speed to the elements.

115

No cussing allowed!

Rev. Clarence Cross had to attend a meeting. On his way to change, he told his wife that the brakes squealed on his old Overland car.

His 10-year-old son, Mortimer, overheard and decided to help. While Rev. Cross changed into his going-to-meeting clothes, Morty oiled the Overland's brakes. He took no credit for his 'good deed' which went undetected until the Rev. Cross arrived at his destination and braked ... the car came to a full stop ... in a creek.

It was many years before Morty confessed, recalls his daughter, Mayone Kelly of Marble Rock. The Rev. Cross' remarks are not recorded, "but he probably laughed because when you're a Pentecostal minister, you don't swear," says Mrs. Kelly.

116

Great Grandmother Running's Butter Tarts

Presented by Georgina Cross, Lansdowne

Ingredients:

1 egg	1 cup of brown sugar
butter (size of walnut)	butter
1 cup of currents or raisins, optional	pastry for tarts
flavor to taste (1/2 tsp of vanilla, 1/8 tsp of salt)	

Method:

Beat until the mixture is full of bubbles. Drop from a teaspoon into pastry lined tins and bake in a quick oven, about 425°F. If you prefer 'drippy' tarts, bake for 12 minutes. For more solid tarts, bake 13 to 15 minutes.

Georgina Cross is the mother of Mayone Kelly whose recipes and stories appear elsewhere in this book. Mrs. Cross is the wife of the late Mortimer Cross who was responsible for oiling the brakes of his father's car (with predictable results) described in the story on this page. Georgina and Mortimer farmed north of Lansdowne, at a location which rejoices to the beautiful name of Dulcemaine. Great Grandmother Running was Morty's grandmother.

Carrot and Pineapple Muffins

Presented by Leanhaven Farms Bed & Breakfast, RR 3, Gananoque

Ingredients:

1 1/2 cups of flour	1 cup of sugar
1 tsp of baking powder	1 tsp of baking soda
1 tsp of cinnamon	1/2 tsp of salt
2/3 cup of salad oil	2 eggs
1 cup of finely grated raw carrots	1 tsp of vanilla
1/2 cup of crushed pineapple with juice	

Method:

Sift the flour, sugar, baking powder, baking soda, cinnamon and salt together in a large bowl. Add the eggs, oil, carrots, pineapple and vanilla. Blend with an electric beater on low speed until all ingredients are moist then beat for 2 minutes on medium speed. Fill greased muffin tins about halfway. Bake at 350°F for 25 minutes.

This recipe yields 24 average-sized muffins.

This recipe comes from Jean McLean who, with husband Ross, operates Leanhaven Farms Bed & Breakfast in their 150-year-old farm house. This is a working farm and guests may tour the farm as they wish. Jean serves her guests a full breakfast and bakes muffins every day. Guests come from Canada, the United States and Europe. Jean has received many requests for the recipe for these delicious muffins.

"Can't it wait?"

Five generations of McLeans have worked the family farm since 1890. The imposing, red brick house was constructed in 1865 with bricks made in a kiln located on the property.

In 1988, Ross and Jean McLean started the Leanhaven Bed & Breakfast to give guests from around the world a taste of farm life. Today, guests may experience many aspects of a working farm. Jean has quite a collection of stories about city folks at the farm.

One such story concerns a guest named Mona who was delighted to attend the birth of a calf. The McLeans named the calf Mona.

Some other guests decided they too wanted to witness a live birth. When roused in the wee hours, they asked if the blessed event could be postponed while they slept in!

117

Sand Hearts

Presented by Dora Shields, Lansdowne

Ingredients:

2 lb (8 cups) of flour	2 lb (4 1/2 cups) of sugar
1 lb (2 cups) of butter	3 eggs
cinnamon	

Method:

Make up into a dough using 2 of the eggs (reserve the third egg) and work until the ingredients are well incorporated. After rolling out and cutting into heart shapes, place the cakes on a pan. Beat the third egg and spread the mixture over the sand hearts with a feather (today we would use a brush) then sprinkle with granulated sugar mixed with finely powdered cinnamon. Bake in 350°F oven for 8 to 10 minutes.

Editors' Note:

To make a smaller quantity, simply cut the ingredients in half except for the 3 eggs ... use 2 instead.

This old recipe comes from a cloth-covered book published early in this century and purchased by Ella Spafford. Ella was born at Berryton, north of Gananoque, in 1892 and died in 1982. Today, the book belongs to Ella's daughter, Dora Shields. Interestingly, it refers to egg yolks as "yelks".

Dora, and her husband, Willis, are life-long residents of the area. Willis has been associated with the Lansdowne Fair Board since 1941.

Chimpanzee Cheesecake

Presented by The Blinkbonnie Motor Lodge, 50 Main Street, Gananoque

Ingredients for the Crust:

1 1/2 cups of Graham cracker crumbs 1/4 cup of granulated sugar

Ingredients for the Cheesecake:

1 lb of cream cheese   1/4 cup of granulated sugar
2 tsp of lemon juice   4 large eggs
1 cup of sour cream   1 cup of mashed bananas*
6 tbsp of melted butter

*approximately 3 medium bananas should yield 1 cup of mashed bananas

Method:

Preheat the oven to 350°F. To make the crust, place the crumbs in a mixing bowl and add the butter and sugar. Blend well. Press the mixture onto the bottom and partly up the sides of a greased 9" springform pan. Smooth the crumb mixture along the bottom to an even thickness. Bake for about 10 minutes at 350°F, remove from the oven and allow to cool before filling.

Preheat the oven to 350°F. To make the filling, beat the cream cheese, sugar and lemon juice together in a large mixing bowl. Add the eggs, one at a time, beating well after each addition. Stir in the sour cream and the mashed bananas and blend well until very smooth. Pour the mixture into the prepared crust and bake for 1 hour. Cool in the oven with the door partly open until the cake is at room temperature. Chill until serving time.

The Blinkbonnie Motor Lodge is owned and operated by the Seal family which also owns and operates The Glen House on the 1,000 Islands Parkway. This recipe was submitted by chef Bernie Lacroix.

Life in the bush

Excerpts from Life in the Clearings Versus the Bush, *by Susanna Moodie, 1853.*

"*Many young men are attracted to the Backwoods by the facilities they present for hunting and fishing ... But hunting and fishing, however fascinating as a wholesome relaxation from labour, will not win bread, or clothe a wife and shivering little ones; and those who give themselves entirely up to such pursuits soon add to these profitless accomplishments the bush vices of smoking and drinking, and quickly throw off those moral restraints upon which their respectability and future welfare mainly depend ... The bush is the most demoralizing place to which an anxious and prudent parent could send a young lad. Freed suddenly from all parental control, and exposed to the contaminating influence of broken-down gentlemen loafers, who hide their pride and poverty in the woods, he joins in their low debauchery ...*"

119

Colder than ice?

Excerpts from an article entitled Ice, *in* Chambers's Edinburgh Journal*, 1846.*

"... *Now, for want of half a moment's reflection ... people in England are very prone to believe that water cannot be made colder than ice; and accordingly, if a good-humoured man succeeds in filling his ice-house, he feels satisfied that his ice is as good as any other man's ice; in short, that ice is ice ... But the truth is, that the temperature of 32 degrees of Fahrenheit – that at which water freezes – is only the commencement of an operation that is almost infinite; for, after its congelation, water is as competent to continue to receive cold as it was when it was fluid ... the extra cold is added to*

Continued on the next page

Lemon Bread
Presented by Nancy Webster, Lansdowne

Ingredients for the Bread:

6 tbsp of shortening	1 cup of white sugar
2 eggs	grated rind of 1 lemon
1/2 cup of milk	1 1/2 cups of all purpose flour
1/2 tsp of baking powder	1/4 tsp of salt
1/2 cup of chopped walnuts	
1/4 cup of drained maraschino cherries	

Ingredients for the Glaze:

1/4 cup of sugar	juice of 1 lemon

Method:

Cream the shortening and sugar and add eggs. Beat this mixture until it is light then add the lemon rind. Sift together the dry ingredients then add gradually to the mixture alternating with the milk. Add the nuts and cherries. Allow the batter to stand in a greased loaf pan (9 1/2" by 5 1/2" by 2 1/2") before putting it into the oven. Bake for 1 hour at 350°F.

While the loaf is still hot, brush with a syrup made with 1/4 cup of sugar and the juice of 1 lemon. Return the loaf to the oven for 1 to 2 minutes.

Nancy Webster and her husband, Eric, and their children own and operate several farms north of Lansdowne. Nancy credits her relative, Janet Michie, with this recipe.

Queen Elizabeth Cake

Presented by Leanhaven Farms Bed & Breakfast, RR 3 Gananoque

Ingredients for the Cake:

1 cup of dates	1 cup of water
1 tsp of soda	1/4 cup of shortening
1 beaten egg	1 cup of white sugar
1 tsp of vanilla	1 1/2 cups of flour
1/4 tsp of salt	1 tsp of baking powder

Ingredients for the Topping:

5 tbsp of brown sugar	1/2 cup of cocoanut
2 tbsp of cream or milk	

Method:

Cut up the dates and add to the water and soda. Let this mixture stand while you mix the shortening, beaten egg, white sugar and vanilla. Now sift and add the flour, salt and baking powder to the shortening-egg mixture. Add the date mixture.

Bake in an 8" square pan for 30 to 35 minutes at 375°F.

Beat the topping ingredients together for five minutes. When the cake is baked, spread the topping mixture over it and return it to the oven to brown.

This recipe comes from Jean McLean at Leanhaven Farms Bed & Breakfast. This is a working farm where guests may tour the farm as they wish.

Continued from previous page and retained by the mass, and thus the temperature of ice falls with the temperature of the air, until, in Lower Canada (now called Quebec–ed.), it occasionally sinks to 40 degrees below zero, or to 72 degrees below the temperature of ice just congealed. "It is evident, therefore, that if two ice-houses were to be filled, the one with the former, say Canada ice, and the other with the latter, say English ice, the difference between the quantity of cold stored up in each would be as appreciable as the difference between a cellar full of gold and a cellar full of copper; in short, the intrinsic value of ice, like that of metals, depends on the investigation of an assayer: that is to say, a cubic foot of Lower Canada ice is infinitely more valuable, or, in other words, it contains infinitely more cold, than a cubic foot of Upper Canada (now Ontario–ed.) ice; which, again, contains more cold than a cubic foot of Wenham ice; which contains infinitely more cold than a cubic foot of English ice; and thus, although each of these four cubic feet of ice has precisely the same shape, they each, as summer approaches, diminish in value – that is to say, they each gradually lose a portion of their cold, until, long before the Lower Canada ice has melted, the English ice has been converted into lukewarm water.

Voyage of the damned

Excerpts from Life in the Clearings Versus the Bush *by Susanna Moodie, 1853.*

"A young relative of mine went down in the steamboat to be present at the Provincial Agricultural Show that was held that year in the town of Brockville, on the St. Lawrence. It was the latter end of September; the weather was wet and stormy, and the boat loaded to the water's edge with cattle and passengers. The promenade decks were filled up with pigs, sheep and oxen. Cows were looking sleepily in at the open doors of the ladies' cabin, and bulls were fastened on the upper deck. Such a motley group of bipeds and quadrupeds were never before huddled into such a narrow space; and, amidst all this din and confusion, a Scotch piper was playing lustily on the bagpipes, greatly to the edification, I've no doubt, of himself and the crowd of animal life around him."

Continued on the next page

122

Quick Rum Cake à la Maison
Presented by Dianne Fisher, Addison

Ingredients:
> 2 tsp of grated orange rind
> 1/2 cup of light rum
> 1 pkg of yellow cake mix to make two layers

Ingredients for Cake Filling:
> 2 pints of whipping cream   stabilizer*
> 1/4 cup of icing sugar   1 tsp of vanilla

*Diane uses Whip It by Oetker. This stabilizes the whipped cream and keeps it from weeping into the cake.

Ingredients for Frosting:
> 6 squares of unsweetened chocolate   1 1/2 cups of icing sugar
> 3 tbsp of hot water   3 eggs
> 1/2 cup of soft butter

Method:
Mix the layer cake according to instructions using the oil, egg additions method on the cake mix package. Add the orange peel and bake in two layer pans. After the cake has cooled, cut each layer in half to make four separate layers. Sprinkle each layer with 2 tbsp of the rum.

Continued on the next page

Continued from the previous page

To make the filling, beat the whipping cream, icing sugar and vanilla together gradually adding the stabilizer as the cream is whipped until it is stiff. Spread the mixture onto layers 1, 2 and 3, stacking the layers as you go. Top it off with the fourth layer. Now the cake is ready to be frosted.

To make the frosting, melt the unsweetened chocolate and beat in the icing sugar and 3 tbsp of hot water until the mixture is smooth and blended. Beat in the eggs one at a time, beating well after each egg is added. Now, add the soft butter and beat the mixture until it is smooth. Ice the cake.

Always store this cake in the refrigerator. Allow it to sit overnight, or for at least several hours, before serving so the flavors blend. Although the icing appears to be runny, it will hold its shape.

Dianne Fisher is a nurse who lives in a house called "Moonwinks". The family boat also bears the name which is taken from a piece of classical music. Dianne says that rum is good only for cooking. One of the editors begs to disagree; rum also is therapeutic. But never let it be said that he argued with a medical professional.

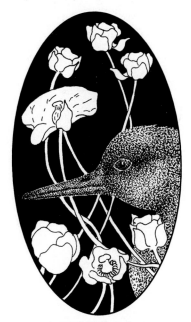

Continued from the previous page

"The night came on very dark and stormy, and many of the women suffered as much from the pitching of the boat as if they had been at sea. The ladies' cabin was crowded to overflowing; every sofa, bed, and chair was occupied; my young friend, who did not feel any inconvenience from the storm, was greatly entertained by the dialogues carried on across the cabin by the women, who were reposing in their berths, and lamenting over the rough weather and their own sufferings in consequence. They were mostly the wives of farmers and respectable mechanics, and the language they used was neither very choice nor grammatical."

Green Tomato Mincemeat

Presented by Irene Warren, Maitland

Ingredients:

4 cups of chopped green tomatoes	6 cups of chopped apples
6 cups of white sugar	2 lb of sultana raisins
4 tsp of cinnamon	2 tsp of salt
2 tsp of allspice	2 tsp of ground cloves
2 tbsp of grated orange rind	1/2 cup of vinegar

Method:

Mix the ingredients well then bring to a boil. Simmer until the mixture is thick, approximately 30 minutes. Pour into sterilized jars and seal at once. Makes four quarts.

Irene Warren was born in Philipsville and lived in Delta for a number of years. Both villages are north of Gananoque. Irene and her husband, Howard, have lived in Maitland since 1972. She is retired from Canada Customs where she worked as a clerk for 12 1/2 years. When Irene is not in the kitchen, cooking, she enjoys watching the ships ply the waters of the St. Lawrence River ... at her front door. This recipe has been in her family for approximately 100 years.

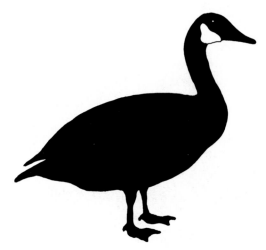

Nature's bounty

Tomatoes were believed to be poisonous and were grown merely as a curiosity until enlightenment set in, about 1850.

Settlers in the new colony grew pumpkins, wheat, squash, melons, beets, carrots and cucumbers for their tables. Some were fortunate to have small orchards and apples were harvested in season. Crab apples and plums were used to make cider and pies – both were popular.

Nature provided her share of bounty in the form of wild gooseberries, currants, raspberries, blackberries and strawberries.

Mandarin Mousse Cake

Presented by Trinity House Inn, 90 Stone Street South, Gananoque

Ingredients:

1 large pkg of orange Jello	1 cup of boiling water
10 egg whites	1/2 cup of sugar
2 pints of whipping cream	pkg of chocolate wafers
1 tbsp of icing sugar	10 oz tin mandarin orange segments
1 thick bar of semi-sweet chocolate	

Method:

You will use three bowls. In bowl one, beat the egg whites until stiff. Add sugar gradually until thoroughly mixed. In bowl two, beat the whipping cream in a chilled bowl until it peaks. In bowl three, dissolve the Jello in the boiling water then fold the contents of bowl one (egg whites) into it. Now fold 3/4 of the whipped cream in bowl two into the mixture.

Line the bottom of a 10" springform pan with chocolate wafers, overlapping to cover the entire surface. Spoon in several large spoonfuls from bowl three into the center of the pan until the mixture almost touches the sides of the pan. Position more chocolate wafers, side by side, around the edge of the pan. Spoon in the rest of the orange cream mixture, making sure the wafers are pressed against the edge of the pan. Smooth out the orange cream mixture.

Add the icing sugar to the remaining whipped cream and mix well. Transfer this to a piping bag with a rosette tip. Form large cream rosettes around the perimeter of the cake. Between each rosette, place a mandarin orange segment. Create chocolate curls by scraping the chocolate bar with the dull side of a large knife. Pile the curls into the center of the cake. Cover and chill overnight. Remove the springform and serve.

Trinity House Inn is an award-winning inn operated by Jacques O'Shea and Brad Garside.

John A. Macdonald

Canada's first prime minister was Sir John A. Macdonald of Kingston. One of his homes, Bellevue House, is a national, historic site open to the public and operated by a branch of the federal government.

Sir John called it "The Pekoe Pagoda" because of its unusual lines. The building was an Italian-style villa of some 15 rooms, when he purchased it in 1848. In those days, it was located on the city's outskirts.

Sir John's son died shortly after the purchase, so the Macdonalds left the house in 1849 to put behind them the sadness encountered there.

125

Ruth's Maple Bran Muffins with Maple Butter Sauce

Presented by The Casablanca Gourmet Bed & Breakfast, Kingston

Ingredients for the Muffins:

2 eggs   1 cup of sour cream or plain yogurt
1 cup of maple syrup   1 cup of flour
1 tsp of baking soda   1 cup of bran flakes
3/4 cup of hazelnuts, coarsely chopped (optional)

Ingredients for the Sauce:

2/3 cup of maple syrup   1/3 cup of butter

Method:

Preheat the oven to 400°F. Grease muffin pans or spray them with a non-stick coating. Beat the eggs briskly with a fork in a large mixing bowl. Add the sour cream or yogurt and 1 cup of maple syrup. Beat this mixture until it is well blended. Add the flour, baking soda and bran flakes and beat well. Stir in the hazelnuts. Spoon the batter into the prepared muffin pans, filling each 3/4 full. Bake about 15 minutes until a straw or skewer comes out clean when stuck into a muffin.

Meanwhile, heat the maple syrup and butter for the sauce in a small saucepan. Stir until the butter is melted and the mixture is blended, then put the sauce in a small bowl. Remove the muffins from the oven, loosen each and remove. Dip the top of each muffin into the sauce then return it to the muffin pan. Let the muffins sit for about 15 minutes before serving. Makes 18 muffins. They may be frozen; simply slip a plastic bag over the pan, wrap in freezer paper or foil and freeze. When serving, reheat for a few minutes at 350°F.

The Casablanca Gourmet Bed & Breakfast offers gourmet dinner and a wide range of cooking classes (hands-on or demonstrations) by Marcel Bahri, a European-trained professional chef.

Frozen Maple Sour Cream

Presented by The Cook not Mad, 110 Clarence Street, Gananoque

Ingredients:

1 cup of sour cream
juice of 1/2 of a fresh lemon
1 oz by weight of white sugar
1/8 lb of hazelnuts*

1/2 cup of maple syrup
3 egg yolks
2 tbsp of maple liqueur

*Hazelnuts are optional but if used, they should be roasted, skinless and coarsely chopped.

Method:

Place the yolks and sugar in a stainless steel bowl. Using an electric mixer, mix at high speed until the mixture is light and fluffy. Continuing to mix at high speed, add the syrup in a steady stream until it is fully incorporated into the mixture. Add the rest of the ingredients (except the nuts, if they are being used) and whip again until well mixed.

Fold in the nuts if desired and process the mixture in an ice cream maker as per the manufacturer's instructions. This 'ice cream' has a lovely, sweet/tart balance and can be used almost anywhere that you might use vanilla ice cream.

The Cook not Mad is owned by Michèle Bussières, Mark Bussières and Nicole LaPrairie. It specializes in regional Canadian cuisine and is smoke free. The restaurant is open for dinner between 5:30 and 8:30 p.m. but call for reservations.

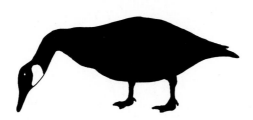

A SWEET SECRET

The Hurons, and other Great Lakes area Indians, depended upon the maple tree for their sweetener. The Indians tapped maples and used evaporation to obtain about one pound of maple sugar for every eight pounds of sap.

The French and the Indians learned from each other. The French discovered how to make maple sugar following the Indian ways. They also learned how to grow Indian corn, squash and kidney beans.

From the French, the Indians obtained technology such as tools and axes.

Once Canada's capital

Kingston played a major role in Canada's development as a country so it seemed only proper to designate it as the capital city when Upper Canada (Ontario) and Lower Canada (Quebec) united in the 19th century.

An appropriate building was completed by 1843 but it had been decided to move Canada's capital, first to Montreal, then Toronto and eventually Ottawa.

As a consequence, Kingston today enjoys the use of a magnificent building as its city hall. The impressive limestone structure, located on the city's waterfront, is a major attraction and tours are conducted during the summer months.

Pineapple Squares
Presented by Dorothy Haesler, Gananoque

Ingredients:

1/2 lb vanilla (or graham) wafers	5 tbsp of melted butter
1/2 cup of butter	2 eggs, well beaten
1 cup of icing sugar	cocoanut or walnuts as required
1 can (19 oz) of pineapple	2 envelopes of Dream Whip

Method:

For the first layer, add 5 tbsp of melted butter to 1/2 lb of wafers and mix well. Spread 3/4 of the mixture on the bottom of a greased 12" by 8" pan and press firmly.

Blend the butter, well beaten eggs and icing sugar and spread this over the crumbs. Now you can add a layer of your preference – cocoanut or walnuts.

Drain the pineapple and spread over the previous layer. Beat two envelopes of Dream Whip and spread that over the pineapple mixture. Finally, sprinkle the remainder of the crumbs on top of the Dream Whip. Refrigerate for 24 hours before serving.

Dorothy Haesler was born in Rockport and grew up on the banks of the St. Lawrence River. She has raised a family of four and today enjoys telling her grandchildren stories of river lore.

Jessie Earl's Doughnuts

Presented by Audrey Tamblyn, Gananoque

Ingredients:

1 cup of white sugar	1 tsp of salt
1 tsp of vanilla	4 tbsp of melted butter
2 eggs	1 cup of milk
3 cups of flour	3 tsp of baking powder
1/2 tsp of baking soda	1 tsp of nutmeg

Method:

Beat together the milk, sugar, salt, vanilla, melted butter and eggs. Add and mix to the flour, baking powder, baking soda and nutmeg. Cover and place the mixture in the refrigerator overnight.

Roll the mixture and cut individual doughnuts using a baking powder tin or a glass. Use a thimble to cut the holes. Drop them in lard heated to 360°F. As soon as each doughnut rises to the top of the lard, turn it and fry for one minute. Turn it again and fry for another minute. Keep the doughnuts moving while in the lard. When cooked, remove to drain on paper towels.

Audrey Tamblyn is a retired beauty shop operator who lives in Gananoque. She learned this recipe from her mother, Jessie Earl. Audrey recalls: "Mother kept these in a large cookie tin on a shelf in the cellarway. They didn't last long – no need for refrigeration."

A wicked marcel wave

Audrey Tamblyn charged 50 cents for what a life-long friend calls "a wicked marcel wave" back in 1932. Hers was the first beauty shop between Gananoque and Brockville.

Audrey was blessed with a wonderful landlord ... in fact, she could call him 'Dad'. W.P. Earl helped his daughter's fledgling business career by making room for her beauty shop on his general store's second floor.

Audrey spent 1931 in Ottawa learning her occupation. She worked for six days a week. In those days, she charged 75 cents for a finger wave.

Downstairs, W.P. Earl sold everything, including a fine pair of overalls for $5. His was one of several stores. In fact, Lansdowne had five grocery stores, three blacksmith shops, three banks and a dance hall during the Depression years.

An 1864 fair

The Lansdowne Fair can trace its origins back to 1864 ... three years before Confederation.

Horse races through the village were a popular feature. The timekeeper perched in an elm tree, time piece in hand. And there were competitions for the best work horses, coach horses and for the best drivers.

And just like today, there were exhibits of vegetables, flowers and fancy work.

By 1875 the fair board leased some land on Lansdowne's north side. This was purchased for $600 in 1884 and has been the fair site ever since. Three more acres were added in 1892 for $350.

130

Luxury No Fail Chocolate Cake
Presented by Marnie Thomson, Greenbush

Ingredients for the Cake:

2 cups of white sugar	2 tsp of vanilla
1/2 cup of margarine	2 cups of flour
1/2 cup of sour milk	2 tbsp of cocoa
3 eggs	1 tsp of baking powder
1/2 tsp of salt	1 tsp of baking soda
1 cup of boiling water	

Ingredients for the Icing:

1 1/2 cups of icing sugar	1 tsp of vanilla
4 tbsp of water	1 tbsp of cocoa
a quantity of margarine, about the size of a golf ball	

Method:

Stir all these ingredients together till mixed then add 1 cup of boiling water all at once. Stir again then pour into a 13" by 9" greased pan and bake at 350°F for about 35 minutes. After the cake has cooled, ice with chocolate icing.

To make the icing, beat the ingredients together and apply.

Marnie says this is an old family recipe that has never failed. The cake is moist and delicious and Marnie credits her mother's wisdom for adding water to enhance the moisture content. Marnie, and her husband, Bruce, live half way between the thriving communities of Greenbush and Rocksprings which are just north of Brockville. They are raising three children, an antique cat, an accident prone dog and eight retired chickens. They spend most of their winter weekends dragging wood from the back swamp to heat their 145-year-old home. Summers are spent ripping weeds from their large vegetable garden as they fight to win that never-ending battle for land rights. They are known throughout their community, and to friends in Gananoque, for an eclectic collection of Volvos which graces their property and for welcome gifts of their excess tomatoes and cucumbers at harvest time.

Burnt Sugar Cake

Presented by Viola Griffin, Marble Rock

Ingredients for the Cake:

1/2 cup of brown sugar	1/2 cup of boiling water
2/3 cup of butter creamed	1 tsp of vanilla
2 eggs, separated	3 cups of flour
3 tsp of baking powder	salt
1 cup of milk	1 cup of white sugar

Ingredients for the Caramel Icing

2 tbsp of butter	1/3 cup of heavy cream
2/3 cup of brown sugar	1/3 tsp of salt
icing sugar	

Method:

Sift the dry ingredients. Separate the eggs and beat the egg whites till stiff. In a saucepan, heat the brown sugar, water and butter. When melted add milk, white sugar and vanilla, stirring constantly. Remove from heat and allow to cool slightly, then add the egg yolks gradually to the mixture. Beat in the dry ingredients gradually until you have a smooth batter. Fold in the beaten egg whites. Pour into a round or square cake pan and bake at 350°F for about 20 to 30 minutes, or until brown. Let cool before icing.

Caramel Icing:

In a saucepan, melt the butter then stir in the brown sugar and salt. Bring to a boil, stirring constantly. Remove from the heat and add the vanilla and enough icing sugar to make a frosting of spreading consistency. Ice the cake and top with walnuts.

Viola and Ross Griffin live on Marble Rock Road, north of Gananoque, on the bank of the Gananoque River. Ross has been a fishing guide all his life. Ross is known for his delicious shore dinners.

A buried treasure?

Excerpts from the History of Leeds and Grenville 1749–1879 *by Thaddeus Leavitt.*

"Prominent among the early settlers was William Larue, better known as Billa Larue. This pioneer located at the mouth of the creek falling into the St. Lawrence (Larue Mills, east of Gananoque–ed.) ... At the point selected, Mr. Larue constructed a dam across the ravine, and furnished himself with an excellent water power. He next built a mill ... At the time of his death, it was currently reported that he was possessed of a very large sum of gold and silver, which he had buried for safe keeping ... Many years have passed ... the original mill has crumbled into dust, but the legend remains, and many were the anxious searches that followed for the hidden gold."

131

A funny farm animal

Cows are herd animals, but, like people, they exhibit the occasional streak of individuality. Ralph and Omar Smith of Lansdowne remember a special Holstein who earned the title, The Magician.

This bovine beauty used her tongue to undo the snap which linked her to the head rail of her milking station. Once liberated, she would stand behind one of the Smith brothers until his sixth sense prodded him to look over his shoulder.

"She'd stand behind you, looking at you as if to say 'I'm loose'," recalls Ralph Smith. "You'd hook her up again and by gosh, you'd get back to milking a cow and here she is standing with her nose stuck up to your face like, 'I'm loose again'."

132

Hasty Pudding
Presented by Martha Landon, Lansdowne

Ingredients for the Pudding:

1 cup of currants or raisins	1/2 tsp of ginger
grated lemon rind	2 whole eggs plus 4 egg yolks
1/2 cup of sugar	1 cup of flour
boiling water or cider	

2 cups of crumbled dried bread or cake crumbs
1/2 cup of finely chopped suet or 1/2 cup of butter cut into bits

Ingredients for the Sauce:

1 tbsp of butter	2 1/2 tsp of flour
3 cups of cider concentrate	2 to 3 tbsp of sugar or honey

Method:

Combine the crumbs and the fat. Stir in the currants or raisins, ginger and lemon rind. Beat the egg yolks, whole eggs and sugar together until frothy and add to the crumb mixture. Blend well and shape into balls the size of an egg. Roll in flour and drop into the boiling water or cider which should be 4" deep. The balls will rise to the top when done in about 20 minutes.

Serve very hot with cider pudding sauce.

To make the sauce, simmer the cider to reduce to one-half of its volume. Melt the butter over low heat and blend in the flour. Add the hot cider gradually, stirring constantly, until the mixture has thickened. Stir in the sugar or honey and simmer for five minutes. Serve hot with the hasty pudding.

Martha Landon and her husband, Byron, live on a dairy farm north of the village of Lansdowne.

One Hundred Cookies

Presented by Beatrice Webster, Lansdowne

A busy little station

Ingredients:

1 cup of white sugar	1 cup of brown sugar
1 cup of butter	1 cup of cooking oil
1 cup of rolled oats	1 cup of cocoanut
1 cup of Rice Krispies	1 tsp of vanilla
1 tsp of baking soda	1/2 tsp of salt
1 egg	1 tsp of cream of tartar
3 1/2 cups of flour	

Method:

Mix the ingredients, drop the dough on to a cookie sheet and press each cookie with a fork. Bake at 350° to 375°F for 12 to 15 minutes.

Beatrice Webster, and her husband, Robert, live on the family farm north of Lansdowne.

Lansdowne's railway station was a hive of activity during the 1920's. Local historian Ralph Smith remembers that more cheddar cheese and baled hay were shipped from Lansdowne than any other Ontario station.

The quality of Leeds County hay is excellent. In fact, the Smith family used to ship hay to the United States from their Goldendale Farm, just north of Lansdowne.

The other 'export' — cheese, came from the many factories throughout the county. Mr. Smith remembers there were 14 factories in 1925 in Front of Leeds and Lansdowne Township.

For trivia collectors, here are their locations: Sand Bay, Warburton, Fairfax, Lansdowne, Tilly, Deerlick, Mitchellville, Selton, Coldbrook (also called Ebenezer), Wilstead, Lorne, South Lake, Cheeseborough, and Taylor. The name Deerlick reflected the curious habit of white tailed deer who licked salt from a particular rock in the area.

Leeds the 'cheesiest'

Leeds County on the St. Lawrence River had the largest cheese production of any Ontario county, at the end of the 19th century.

According to Canada's 1871 census, there was only one cheese factory in the Front of Leeds and Lansdowne Township. Some 20 years later, one or two cheese factories were to be found on each concession road.

Many cheese factories were patron-owned but inevitably were sold to the cheesemaker himself. Cheesemakers were specialists who learned their trade at a dairy school, originally at Kingston. Eventually it moved to Kemptville. A few learned the old fashioned way by working with a trained cheesemaker.

Whipped Shortbread
Presented by Vaida Truesdell, Lansdowne

Ingredients:

2 cups of soft butter	1 cup of icing sugar
1/2 cup of corn starch	a pinch of salt
3 cups of flour	

Method:

Whip the butter until it is creamy and slowly add the sugar, corn starch and flour. Whip for 12 to 15 minutes with a slow beater.

Drop from a teaspoon and put small pieces of red or green cherries on top. Bake at 350°F until the shortbread is brown.

Vaida Truesdell worked for the Ontario government at a tourism information center. Today, she is retired and lives in Lansdowne.

Lemon Sponge Pie

Presented by Nancy Webster, Lansdowne

Ingredients:

1 cup of white sugar
2 egg yolks
a pinch of salt
1 cup of sweet milk
single pie crust

1/4 cup of flour
1 tbsp of butter
1 lemon
2 well beaten egg whites

Method:

Mix the sugar, flour, egg yolks, butter and salt then add the juice of the lemon and its grated rind, the milk and well beaten egg whites. Pour the mixture into an unbaked pie shell and bake in a fairly hot oven until set and brown.

Nancy Webster, and her husband, Eric, lives on a farm north of Lansdowne.

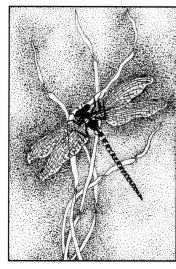

A grave offence

Buying a body was a time-honored way for medical students to acquire cadavers. Robbing a grave was another.

Back in 1903, a Kingston doctor, assisted by a law student, snatched the body of a Lansdowne woman from her grave. She had been buried that afternoon. But someone fingered the grave robbers who were apprehended in Gananoque, on their way back to Kingston.

After their court appointment and subsequent delays to two promising careers, the law student redeemed himself to become a judge. But recidivism claimed the doctor who lapsed into antisocial behaviour; he entered the political arena.

The effluxion of time

Five generations of Robert Webster's family have tilled this rich soil, north of Lansdowne. Robert's great, great, grandfather, also named Robert, was born in Ireland in 1788, one of a family of 19. He emigrated to Canada and was married at Kingston's St. George's Cathedral in 1820.

His son, and the present Robert's great grandfather, had built the family home by 1874 although the farm had been in the family since 1853. The bricks for the house were made on the spot. He used to walk to Kingston bearing a sack of wheat to be ground into flour.

His son, and Robert's father, started the first registered holstein herd in Leeds County in 1910 and the Websters have raised and milked the finest holsteins ever since. Robert's wife, Beatrice, née McCready is descended from United Empire Loyalists. Her family arrived in 1793 and she too is fifth generation.

Chocolate Cake
Presented by Beatrice Webster, Lansdowne

Ingredients:

2 cups of flour
2 tsp of baking powder
1/2 cup of shortening
1 1/2 cups of white sugar
1 tbsp of vanilla
1/2 tsp of salt

2 tsp of baking soda
1/2 cup (very scant) of cocoa
2 eggs
1/2 cup of sour milk
1 cup of boiling water

Method:

Cream the shortening then add the sugar and beat. Add the eggs and beat again.

In a separate bowl, mix the flour, baking soda, baking powder, salt and cocoa. In another bowl, add the vanilla to the sour milk. Now, combine and mix alternately the flour mixture and sour milk mixture into the shortening and sugar mixture. Add the boiling water last; this will make the batter very thin. Pour the mixture into an 8" by 11" pyrex pan and bake at 350°F for 25 to 30 minutes.

Beatrice Webster and her husband, Robert, live on the family farm north of Lansdowne. This recipe comes from her mother, Mariam McCready née Tye.

Peach Almond Pie

Presented by Chez Piggy Restaurant, 68-R Princess Street, Kingston

Ingredients for the Filling:

8 to 12 ripe peaches	1/4 cup of flour
1 tsp of cinnamon	1/2 cup of sugar
6 tbsp of half and half cream	1/2 cup of sour cream

Ingredients for the Topping:

1/2 cup of brown sugar	1/4 cup of butter, cut into pieces
1/4 cup of flour	1 tsp of cinnamon
1/2 cup of sliced almonds	

single pastry for a 9" pie

Method:

Preheat the oven to 400°F. Line a 9" pie pan with the dough and bake blind for 12 minutes. Let the pie shell cool.

To make the filling, blanch, peel and slice the peaches then place them in a bowl. Combine the flour, sugar and cinnamon and sprinkle over the peaches. Stir in the sour cream and half and half and fill the cooled crust with the mixture.

To make the topping, preheat the oven to 350°F. Crumble together the sugar, butter, flour and cinnamon. Mix in the almonds and sprinkle the crumbs over the peach filling. Bake for 55 minutes. Makes one pie.

Chez Piggy's imaginative, international cuisine is complemented by an extensive wine list. All desserts and breads are baked daily at its bakery, Pan Chancho, at 70 Johnson Street. Many of Chez Piggy's desserts and other menu items are available there for take-out as well as a wide selection of salads, patés and imported cheeses. The chef is Victoria Newbury; co-owners are Rose Richardson and Zal Yanovsky.

This is progress?

Excerpt from the History of Leeds and Grenville 1749–1879 *by Thaddeus Leavitt.*

"It is related that about the year 1810, Peter Cole walked from Cole's Ferry to Kingston, where he took the mail from Toronto on his back, and proceeded through the woods to Montreal (about 180 miles–ed.). At that place he received the mail for Toronto (the accumulation for one month), it only weighing sixty pounds, and with this he trudged back to Kingston. The entire trip was made in fourteen days, and for the journey he received $15."

Ralph Smith of Lansdowne adds a recollection from the 1920's. He used to mail a letter at 10 p.m. in Lansdowne to a cousin in Montreal. She received it next morning before she went to work.

Fast forward to the present: a first class letter has been known to require 13 days to cover the 32 miles between Brockville and Gananoque. Such is progress.

Historic Bridge Island

The St. Lawrence River was the lifeline of 19th century Upper Canada (present day Ontario). All military and civilian supplies were transported from Montreal to Kingston via the river.

Fear that the Americans might try to block the passage of materiel during the War of 1812–14 prompted the fortification of Bridge Island, now called Chimney Island, near Mallorytown Landing. This fort served as a base for British gunboats. The blockhouse was completed early in 1814 and a circular battery with an 18 pounder cannon was constructed. These defences fell into disrepair soon after the war.

Another blockhouse was situated at Gananoque and four 24 pounder carronades, called 'smashers' because of their awesome destructive power, were placed on the upper storey. These two-storey forts were constructed of stone below and logs above. The upper storey overhung the lower and both levels were pierced with firing ports.

138

Hello Dollies
Presented by Katherine Warren, Gananoque

Ingredients:

1/2 cup of melted butter	1 cup of crushed graham crackers
1 cup of cocoanut	1 small pkg of chocolate chips
1/2 cup of nuts	1 can of condensed milk

Method:

Place in a pan exactly as listed. Do not mix. Pour the condensed milk over the mixture. Bake in a moderate oven (325°F) for 30 to 40 minutes. Cut in squares.

This recipe comes from Katherine's mother, the late Margaret Crouch, who was head waitress for 28 years at Gananoque's Golden Apple Restaurant.

Lazy Squares

Presented by Viola Griffin, Marble Rock

Ingredients:

1/2 cup of butter
1 pkg of chocolate chips
1 cup of cocoanut
1 cup of chopped walnuts

1 cup of crushed graham wafers
1 pkg of butterscotch chips
1 can of sweet condensed milk

Method:

Melt the butter and pour into a 9" by 13" pan. Sprinkle in the crushed graham wafers, the chocolate and butterscotch chips. Add the rest of the ingredients, mix, then bake at 350°F until brown. This is a very rich mixture so cut into small squares.

Viola Griffin, and her husband, Ross, live on the bank of the Gananoque River at Marble Rock.

... and no taxes!

Excerpt from a memoir of Adiel Sherwood in the History of Leeds and Grenville 1749–1879 *by Thaddeus Leavitt.*

"While many difficulties were encountered in the early settlement (around the 1780's), yet we realized many advantages. We were always supplied with venison; deer were very plentiful, partridge and pigeons in abundance, plenty of fish for all who wished to catch them, no taxes to pay, and an abundance of wood at our doors. Although deprived of many kinds of fruit, we obtained the natural productions of the country – strawberries, raspberries, gooseberries, blackberries, and plenty of red plums. The cranberries were found in abundance in the marshes."

History and heritage

Beecher House, the Brockville Museum, is named for Isaac Beecher who was the first known occupant of the building. He purchased the property in 1824. In 1840, he constructed an addition which is now the main house.

In 1867, the Central Canada Coal Company acquired the building. For the next 100 years the company carried on its business from the premises and surrounding industrial buildings.

In 1977, the City of Brockville obtained Beecher House as the permanent home of the Brockville Museum. Today, the museum has two galleries designed for temporary exhibits and a permanent installation called The River City *devoted to Brockville history.*

Central to the exhibit is a lovingly restored St. Lawrence Skiff built here in the 1890's by the Sauvé brothers. A photographic panorama of the river provides an informative backdrop for the skiff exhibit.

Homemade Ice Cream
Presented by The Brockville Museum, 5 Henry Street, Brockville

Editors' Note:
Bonnie Burke, the museum's education and public programmer, uses this recipe and a hand-powered ice cream maker to show children what goes into making this favorite treat.

Ingredients:

1 cup of white sugar	2 tbsp of vanilla
1 tsp of salt	2 liters of half and half cream
10 lb of ice in small cubes	rock salt

Method:
Mix the sugar, vanilla, salt and cream in a mixing bowl then empty this into an ice cream maker. Layer ice cubes one quarter of the way up the container and cover with a thin layer of rock salt. Keep alternating the ice and rock salt until the container is level with the top of the inner bowl.

It takes about 20 minutes of hand cranking to turn the mixture into ice cream.

Bonnie Burke of the Brockville Museum says this recipe shows children how much time and effort goes into preparing this treat. This is part of the museum's program called 19th Century Children at Play. *Bonnie says this activity is used to enhance the education program. The Brockville Museum is located near the city's scenic waterfront. It features local historical archives, changing thematic exhibits, a picnic area and more. With a new addition in 1995, the museum has doubled in size.*

Maple Syrup Pie

Presented by Beatrice Webster, Lansdowne

Ingredients:

1 baked 8" pie shell	1 cup of maple syrup
1/2 cup of water	2 tbsp of flour (not heaping)
1 tbsp of cornstarch	2 separated eggs
1/2 tsp of salt	1 tsp of vanilla
1 tbsp of butter	1/4 cup of water
2 tbsp of icing sugar	

Method:

Heat the maple syrup and the 1/2 cup of water. Mix the flour, cornstarch and 1/4 cup of water. Add a little of the hot maple syrup to the flour mixture and stir until smooth. Return it to the pan and cook until it is thick and clear, stirring constantly. Beat the egg yolks and add a little of the hot mixture. Beat smooth and return it to the heat and cook for a few minutes. Pour the filling into the pie shell. Beat egg whites until stiff. Fold in the icing sugar and spoon the meringue over the filling. Bake at 375°F until the meringue is delicately browned, about 10 minutes.

Beatrice and Robert Webster live on the family dairy farm north of Lansdowne where they raise holstein cattle.

The first 'harvest'

Excerpts from Chambers's Edinburgh Journal, *1847, concerning new settlers in the early part of the 19th century.*

" ... *At last spring came. In March they began to make maple-sugar, the very first thing their land had yielded them in the way of eatables. They now bored auger-holes in the sugar-maple trees, and putting small wooden spouts in the holes, they caught the sap, which fell in small rude troughs, cut out of blocks of wood. This was boiled, and made into sugar, a great luxury indeed for them all.*"

141

A day's entertainment

Excerpts from Life in the Clearings Versus the Bush, *by Susanna Moodie, 1853, concerning a visit to Kingston Penitentiary.*

"It is about three years ago that I paid a visit with my husband to the Penitentiary, and went over every part of it. I must own that I felt a greater curiosity to see the convicts than the prison which contained them, and my wishes were completely gratified ... The silence system is maintained here, no conversation being allowed between the prisoners ... the overseers were small delicate-looking men; but such is the force of habit, and the want of moral courage which generally accompanies guilt, that a word or a look from these men was sufficient to keep them (convicts–ed.) *at work ..."*

Continued on the next page

Pumpkin Jelly Roll

Presented by Mary Joan Barrett, 1,000 Islands Parkway

Ingredients for the Cake:

1 cup + 2 tbsp of all purpose flour   1 tsp of baking powder
2 tsp of cinnamon   1 tsp of ground ginger
1/2 tsp of ground nutmeg   1/2 tsp of salt
3 eggs*   1 cup of sugar
2/3 cup of pumpkin purée   1 tsp of orange juice
1/4 cup of chopped almonds

Ingredients for the Filling:

1 cup of icing sugar   1 small pkg of cream cheese*
2 tbsp of orange cream liqueur   1/2 tsp of vanilla extract
1 tbsp of grated orange rind   1 cup of whipping cream
1 tsp of icing sugar

*at room temperature

Method:

Preheat the oven to 325°F and grease a 15" by 10" by 3/4" jelly roll pan and line it with wax paper. Grease the paper also.

In a medium bowl, sift together the dry ingredients. In a large bowl, beat the eggs until they are light and fluffy. Gradually add the sugar and continue to beat the mixture until it is pale yellow and slowly dissolving ribbons form when the egg beater is lifted from the bowl. Mix in the pumpkin and orange juice then fold in the sifted, dry ingredients.

Continued on the next page

Continued from previous page

Spread the batter evenly over the bottom of the pan. Top evenly with the chopped almonds and bake 25 minutes or until a toothpick inserted in the center of the cake comes out clean. Cool the cake on a rack.

To make the filling, beat until smooth the sugar, cream cheese, liqueur, vanilla and orange rind in a medium sized bowl with an electric mixer. Beat the whipping cream in a separate bowl until soft peaks form. Fold the cheese mixture into the whipped cream and refrigerate for 15 minutes.

To prepare the jelly roll, invert the cake on a damp tea towel. Peel off the paper and spread the filling over the cake leaving a 1/2" border. Roll up the cake starting at one long edge and using the towel as an aid. Carefully lay the jelly roll on a long serving plate and dust lightly with the balance of the icing sugar.

This recipe may be prepared eight hours ahead of time and refrigerated. Let it stand at room temperature for 10 minutes before serving. This elegant dessert is ideal for a springtime dinner party.

Mary Joan Barrett is the author of In Praise of Pumpkins *published by History Unlimited, 192 Old River Road, RR # 2, Mallorytown, Ontario, K0E 1R0. This delightful cookbook contains a wealth of recipes including some pioneer dishes, soups, main courses, Thanksgiving treats, cakes and pies, soups, Cinderella desserts and kids' recipes, and all feature the pumpkin.*

Continued from the previous page

"Executions in Canada are so rare, even for murder, that many atrocious criminals are found within these walls – men and women – who could not possibly have escaped the gallows in England ... I could not help thinking, while watching these men in their comfortable dresses, taking their wholesome, well-cooked meal, how much better they were fed and lodged than thousands of honest industrious men, who had to maintain large families upon a crust of bread, in the great manufacturing cities at home ... I must now introduce my reader to the female inmates of this house of woe and crime. At the time of my visit, there were only forty women in the Penitentiary. This speaks much for the superior moral training of the feebler sex."

Editors' Note: Visitors were charged for the chance to see the convicts. In 1836, a member of the "feebler sex" paid 7 1/2 pence; men, 1 shilling 3 pence.

143

Teddie and Nellie

Lilian Griffin, who was born early in this century, remembers bundling her children into a sleigh behind her husband's two, huge draft horse, Teddie and Nellie. Off they went in search of the perfect Christmas tree, with the horses breaking a trail through the deep snow.

Horses played a major role in Lilian's life. A two-horse-powered buggy or cutter was a dependable means of transportation in her day. She recalls how teams of horses were used to haul ice blocks, cut from Gananoque Lake, to ice houses. These blocks were packed in sawdust until needed for the icebox. Many homes enjoyed Mother Nature's natural refrigeration all summer, in those days before electricity.

To this day, Lilian has a special love of horses and is a special fan of Olympian Ian Millar and his horse, Big Ben.

Easy Pumpkin Pie
Presented by Pat Lackie, Lansdowne

Ingredients:

double pie crust	1 tbsp of flour
1 tbsp of brown sugar	pumpkin sliced like an apple
3/4 cup of brown sugar	butter
1/2 tsp of cinnamon	1/2 tsp of nutmeg
1/2 tsp of allspice	

Method:

Begin by sprinkling 1 tbsp of flour and 1 tbsp of brown sugar in a pie pan. Cover with the bottom crust and fill with pumpkin. Sprinkle 1 tbsp of flour and 3/4 cup of brown sugar on top. Add a chunk of butter and the spices then fit the top crust. Bake for 1 hour at 350°F.

Pat Lackie has been a teacher and a cook at a resort. Today, she is retired and lives in Lansdowne.

Dried Apple Cake

Presented by Martha Landon, Lansdowne

Ingredients:

1 cup of dried apples	1 cup of molasses
2/3 cup of sour cream	1 cup of granulated sugar
1 egg	1 3/4 cups of all purpose flour
2 tsp of baking soda	1 tsp of cinnamon
1/2 tsp of cloves or allspice	1/2 tsp of salt

Method:

Place the dried apples in a bowl and add cold water to cover them. Let this set in a cool place overnight, or, for at least six hours.

In the morning, drain and chop the apples finely. Place them in a saucepan with the molasses and when this begins to simmer, cook for 20 minutes. Allow this mixture to cool.

Combine the cream, sugar and egg and beat until smooth. Combine the dry ingredients and sift together several times. Beat the liquids into the dry ingredients until the mixture is smooth. Stir in the fruit and molasses mixture.

Pour the mixture into a buttered, floured 8 1/4" by 4 1/4" loaf pan and bake in a moderate over at 350°F for one hour.

This is a very tasty dessert. Dried apricots or prunes may be substituted for the apples to add variety to your menu.

Serves 6 to 8.

Martha and Byron Landon live on a dairy farm near the village of Lansdowne.

Social life back when

"If you wanted to get the news, you went to the barber shop," recalls Ralph Smith, Lansdowne area farmer and historian. "The barber knew everything because he listened to everybody who was talking so he was the center for any inquiries."

Ralph recalls that on Saturday nights the young men collected the young women and drove around. This was followed by the obligatory visit to the ice cream parlor before going home.

Social life in the 1920's and 1930's centered as well on stores' back rooms. Most were equipped with nail keg seats "where there was always a place for two or three fellas to sit down and have a yak on Saturday night. Then they got radios and the fellas would listen to the hockey matches on those first radios."

Ralph remembers one elderly man who relied upon a funnel and a length of rubber tubing to create an ear trumpet to help him hear those early broadcasts.

LITERARY CRITICISM

Excerpt from Chambers's Edinburgh Journal, 1846.

"The Emigrant *by Sir Francis Head, if not the most amusing, is at least one of the most curious literary compounds which have for some time issued from the press. By its eccentric and clever author it is candidly compared to a crow – 'a small lump of carrion, and two or three handfuls of feathers;' the carrion being certain chapters on Canadian politics, and the feathers the lighter sketches by which the said disquisitions are enabled to take flight ... His homilies on the Canadian rebellion, and maunderings on the prospective ruin of the colonists by the introduction of 'responsible government,' borne up though they be with a good many jokes, would assuredly have had little chance of popularity, unless blended with a variety of short and spirited sketches, suitable to the present craving for that species of material."*

Snicker Doodles
Presented by Katherine Warren, Gananoque

Ingredients:

1/2 cup of sifted cake flour	1/8 tsp of salt
1/2 tsp double acting baking powder	5 tbsp of melted butter
1/2 cup of sugar	2 well beaten eggs
1/4 tsp of vanilla	3 tbsp of sugar
1/4 tsp of cinnamon	
1/2 cup of finely chopped walnut meats	

Method:

Sift the flour once then add the baking powder and salt and sift again. Mix the butter and sugar, add the eggs and vanilla and mix lightly. Stir in the flour. Pour the mixture into a greased 8" by 8" by 2" pan.

Combine the sugar and cinnamon and sprinkle over top then cover with chopped nuts. Bake in a moderate oven at 375°F for 25 minutes or until done. Cut into squares and serve either warm or cold.

This is another recipe from Katherine's mother, Margaret Crouch. She was the head waitress at the Golden Apple Restaurant for 28 years. During that time, she collected recipes from many of her fellow employees. These recipes are among many contained in a scribbler which is in Katherine's possession.

Molasses Moons

Presented by Peggy Delaney, Gananoque

Ingredients:

2 cups of sifted flour
1 tsp of baking powder
1 tsp of ground cloves
3/4 cup of shortening
4 tbsp of molasses

1 tsp of baking soda
1 tsp of cinnamon
1 tsp of ginger
1 cup of white sugar
1 egg

Method:

Cream the shortening, sugar and molasses and add the egg. In a separate bowl, mix the dry ingredients then add to the first mixture and mix well.

Use your hands to form balls which are about 1" in diameter. Roll the balls in the white sugar and place them on a greased baking sheet, about 2" apart. Press lightly with a fork and bake at 325°F for 15 minutes.

Peggy Delaney grew up on a farm near the village of Lansdowne; today she lives in Gananoque. Peggy says these cookies are so good that her son once tried to make some. On the assumption that more is better, he doubled the quantities and mixed the batter in a pail. His math was not quite up to snuff ... instead of doubling, he multiplied by eight. Peggy could not bear the thought of so much going to waste so she encouraged him to finish the job. "There were enough cookies to cover the dining room table," she recalls, years later.

Automotive memories

Here is a partial list of automobiles which Lansdowne historian, Ralph Smith, remembers from about 1918 onwards. How many can you remember?

Stutz	*Daimler*	*Woolsey*
MG	*Triumph*	*Brisco*
Model A	*Model T*	*Tudhope*
Mitchell	*Overland*	*Willys*
Whippet	*Durant*	*Star*
Frontenac	*Ace*	*Maxwell*
Moon	*Jordan*	*Page*
Kaiser	*Reo*	*Chandler*
Hupmobile	*Erskine*	*Wolverine*
Oakland	*Marquette*	*Fraser*
Essex	*Legare*	*Auburn*
Cord	*Terraplane*	*La Salle*

How about the Stanley Steamer? Or the Brooks Steamer? Do you remember the Pierce-Arrow? Gray-Dort? Graham-Paige? Brockville Atlas? McLaughlin? Flying Cloud V-12?

147

Dream River

Wind-silvered willows hedge the stream,
And all within is hushed and cool.
The water, in an endless dream,
Goes sliding down from pool to pool.
And every pool a sapphire is,
From shadowy deep to sunlit edge,
Ribboned around with irises
And cleft with emerald spears of sedge.

O, every morn the winds are stilled,
The sunlight falls in amber bars.
O, every night the pools are filled
With silver bede of shaken stars.
O, every morn the sparrow flings
His elfin trills athwart the hush,
And here unseen at eve there sings
One crystal-throated hermit thrush.

MARJORIE PICKTHALL
1883–1922